CAMBRIDGE LATIN TEXTS

VIRGIL: SELECTIONS FROM AEN

CAMBRIDGE LATIN TEXTS

VIRGIL

SELECTIONS FROM AENEID IV

with a further selection from the English
translation of C. Day Lewis

J. V. MUIR

University of London King's College

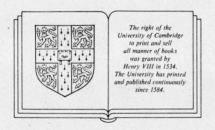

The right of the
University of Cambridge
to print and sell
all manner of books
was granted by
Henry VIII in 1534.
The University has printed
and published continuously
since 1584.

CAMBRIDGE UNIVERSITY PRESS

CAMBRIDGE

NEW YORK   NEW ROCHELLE

MELBOURNE   SYDNEY

Published by the Press Syndicate of the University of Cambridge
The Pitt Building, Trumpington Street, Cambridge CB2 1RP
32 East 57th Street, New York, NY 10022, USA
10 Stamford Road, Oakleigh, Melbourne 3166, Australia

© Cambridge University Press 1977

ISBN 0 521 21581 1   limp

First published 1977
Fifth printing 1987

Printed in Great Britain at the
University Press, Cambridge

ACKNOWLEDGEMENTS

The Latin text is taken from the Oxford Classical Text, *The Complete Works of Virgil*, edited by R. A. B. Mynors, and is reproduced by permission of The Clarendon Press, Oxford. © 1969 Oxford University Press.

The English text is taken from *The Aeneid of Virgil*, translated by C. Day Lewis, and is reproduced by permission of The Executors of the Estate of C. Day Lewis and the Hogarth Press, and A. D. Peters & Co. Ltd.

The cover photograph, a detail from the mosaic floor of the frigidarium of the villa at Low Ham in Somerset, is reproduced by permission of Somerset County Museum.

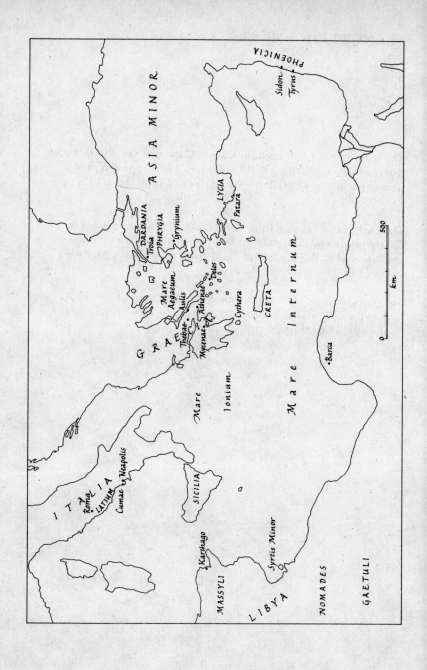

PREFACE

Aeneas together with his father, Anchises, his son, Ascanius, and a small band of Trojans managed to escape from Troy after its capture and destruction by the Greeks. They met with many trials and adventures and finally reached Sicily where Aeneas' father, who had been a great support to him, died. The Trojans put to sea again and a storm drove them to the North African coast near the newly-founded city of Carthage where the beautiful queen, Dido, was making a new home for herself and her people (she had lived in Tyre with her husband, Sychaeus, but Sychaeus had been murdered by her brother). The Trojans were at once welcomed to Carthage and asked to join the new settlement on equal terms. Dido invited Aeneas to a great banquet in the palace where she asked him to tell the story of the horrors of Troy and the Trojans' subsequent wanderings. Aeneas was reluctant to re-live so much sorrow but finally agreed, holding his audience, and especially Dido, spell-bound with his tale. At the end of Book III his story is finished and the long evening of the banquet is just over.

at regina gravi iamdudum saucia cura
vulnus alit venis et caeco carpitur igni.
multa viri virtus animo multusque recursat
gentis honos: haerent infixi pectore vultus
verbaque nec placidam membris dat cura quietem.   5
postera Phoebea lustrabat lampade terras
umentemque Aurora polo dimoverat umbram,
cum sic unanimam adloquitur male sana sororem:
' Anna soror, quae me suspensam insomnia terrent!
quis novus hic nostris successit sedibus hospes,   10
quem sese ore ferens, quam forti pectore et armis!
credo equidem, nec vana fides, genus esse deorum.
degeneres animos timor arguit. heu, quibus ille
iactatus fatis! quae bella exhausta canebat!
si mihi non animo fixum immotumque sederet   15

2

igni – pire
alit – noun?),

iamdūdum for a long time now
saucius wounded, hurt
cūra, f. concern, distress
gravi... curā by a deep concern
vēna, f. vein, *here* = life-blood
vulnus alit venis feeds the wound with her life-blood
caecus blind, hidden
carpere pluck, wear away
multa...multus *here* = often...often
recursāre run back, return
multa viri virtus animo (recursat) multusque...
īnfīxus fastened in, implanted
vultus, m. face, expression
6 **Phoebēus** of Apollo, the sun-god
lūstrāre purify, range over
ūmēns dank
Aurōra, f. Aurora, goddess of the dawn
polus, m. axis, sky
dīmovēre move aside, dispel
umbra, f. shadow, darkness
*postera Aurora Phoebeā lampade lustrabat terras umentemque umbram
    polo dimoverat*
ūnanimus of one mind, dearly loved
male sānus scarcely sane, distraught
(regina) male sana... adloquitur
quae...īnsomnia...! what dreams...!
suspēnsus anxious, on edge
10 **succēdere + Form C (dative)** arrive, enter
sēdēs, f. seat, home
quis novus hic... successit... hospes! what a man is this new guest who
    has entered...!
quem sēsē ōre ferēns! what an expression he has! *lit.* bearing himself as
    what in his expression
equidem indeed
vānus groundless, without reason
fidēs, f. belief
nec vana (est mea) fides
dēgener ignoble, inferior
arguere prove, reveal
fātum, n. fate
exhaustus draincd to the dregs, seen through to the end
canere sing, describe
15 **sī...nōn...sedēret nē...vellem** if it were not settled...that I should
    refuse

3

ne cui me vinclo vellem sociare iugali,
postquam primus amor deceptam morte fefellit;
si non pertaesum thalami taedaeque fuisset,
huic uni forsan potui succumbere culpae.
Anna (fatebor enim) miseri post fata Sychaei   20
coniugis et sparsos fraterna caede penates
solus hic inflexit sensus animumque labantem
impulit. agnosco veteris vestigia flammae.
sed mihi vel tellus optem prius ima dehiscat
vel pater omnipotens adigat me fulmine ad umbras,   25
pallentes umbras Erebo noctemque profundam,
ante, pudor, quam te violo aut tua iura resolvo.
ille meos, primus qui me sibi iunxit, amores
abstulit; ille habeat secum servetque sepulcro.'
sic effata sinum lacrimis implevit obortis.   30

Anna replied:–
            You are dearer to me than the light of day.
Must you go on wasting your youth in mourning and solitude,
Never to know the blessings of love, the delight of children?
Do you think that ashes, or ghosts underground, can mind about such
        things?
I know that in Libya, yes, and in Tyre before it, no wooers
Could touch your atrophied heart: Iarbas was rejected
And other lords of Africa, the breeding-ground of the great.
Very well: but when love comes, and pleases, why fight against it?
Besides, you should think of the nations whose land you have settled in –
Threatening encirclement are the Gaetuli, indomitable
In war, the Numidians (no bridle for them), the unfriendly Syrtes;
On your other frontier, a waterless desert and the far-raging
Barcaei: I need not mention the prospect of Tyrian aggression,
Your brother's menacing attitude.
I hold it was providential indeed, and Juno willed it,
That hither the Trojan fleet should have made their way. Oh, sister,
Married to such a man, what a city you'll see, what a kingdom
Established here! With the Trojans as our comrades in arms,
What heights of glory will not we Carthaginians soar to!
Only solicit the gods' favour, perform the due rites,

4

cui:quis anyone
vinclō = vinculō: vinculum, n. bond
iugālī: iugālis of marriage
ne vellem me cui sociare vinclo iugali
dēceptus cheated, bereaved
sī nōn pertaesum...fuisset + Form D (genitive) if I had not wearied of
thalamus, m. room, bridal chamber
forsan perhaps
succumbere + Form C (dative) give way to
culpa, f. fault, source of temptation
20 Sychaeus, m. Sychaeus, Dido's first husband
frāternus of a brother, of a relation
post fata miseri Sychaei coniugis et (post) sparsos...penates after the
    death (*lit.* fate) of poor Sychaeus, my husband, and after our home
    was bespattered with the murder of a relative
īnflexit: īnflectere bend, alter
labāre totter, waver
impulit: impellere strike, make an impression on
flamma, f. flame, passion
prius optem vel tellus ima mihi dehiscat vel...antequam... I should
    prefer that either the earth should gape open for me to its lowest
    depths (*lit.* the lowest earth should gape open) or...before...
25 adigere drive, force
fulmen, n. thunderbolt
ad umbrās to the shades = to the place of the shades
Erebus, m. the Underworld
pudor, m. conscience
violāre violate, dishonour
resolvere loosen, break
abstulit: auferre take away
ille habeat (meos amores)
30 effārī speak out, reveal one's thoughts
sinus, m. bosom, fold of dress
obortus risen up, welling up

51 And plying our guest with attentions, spin a web to delay him,
   While out at sea the winter runs wild and Orion is stormy,
   While his ships are in bad repair, while the weather is unacquiescent.

      his dictis impenso animum flammavit amore
   spemque dedit dubiae menti solvitque pudorem.   55
   principio delubra adeunt pacemque per aras
   exquirunt; mactant lectas de more bidentes
   legiferae Cereri Phoeboque patrique Lyaeo,
   Iunoni ante omnes, cui vincla iugalia curae.
   ipsa tenens dextra pateram pulcherrima Dido   60
   candentis vaccae media inter cornua fundit,
   aut ante ora deum pingues spatiatur ad aras,
   instauratque diem donis, pecudumque reclusis
   pectoribus inhians spirantia consulit exta.
   heu, vatum ignarae mentes! quid vota furentem,   65
   quid delubra iuvant? est molles flamma medullas
   interea et tacitum vivit sub pectore vulnus.
   uritur infelix Dido totaque vagatur

impēnsus heavy, great
55 **dubius** uncertain, wavering
solvit . . . pudōrem eased her conscience, *lit.* loosened her conscience
prīncipiō in the beginning, first
dēlūbrum, n. shrine
pāx, f. peace, *here* = divine sanction
per ārās by going from altar to altar
exquīrere seek
mactāre sacrifice
lēctus chosen
dē mōre in the proper fashion
bidēns, f. a young sheep
lēgifer law-giving
Cerēs, f. the goddess Ceres
Phoebus, m. the god Apollo
Lyaeus, m. the Deliverer, i. e. the god Bacchus
Iūnō, f. the goddess Juno
cui vincla iugalia (*sunt*) *curae* who is responsible for the bonds of
  marriage
60 **dextra, f.** right hand
ipsa pulcherrima Dido pateram dextrā tenens
candēns white
vacca, f. cow
fundere pour (an offering)
ōs, n. face, presence
deum = deōrum
pinguis well-fed, rich
spatiārī walk solemnly
īnstaurāre begin a ceremony again, renew
instaurat . . . diem donis keeps renewing her offerings of gifts during the
  day, *lit.* renews the day with her gifts
pecus, f. animal
reclūsus opened up, open
inhiāre peer into
spīrāre breathe, live
cōnsulere consult, examine
exta, n.pl. entrails
65 |**vātēs, m.f.** soothsayer, priest
quid? *here* = how?
vōtum, n. prayer, offering
ēst: ēsse eat
medulla, f. marrow of the bones
molles . . . medullas
tacitus silent, secret
sub + Form E (ablative) beneath
vagārī wander

7

urbe furens, qualis coniecta cerva sagitta,
quam procul incautam nemora inter Cresia fixit   70
pastor agens telis liquitque volatile ferrum
nescius: illa fuga silvas saltusque peragrat
Dictaeos; haeret lateri letalis harundo.
nunc media Aenean secum per moenia ducit
Sidoniasque ostentat opes urbemque paratam,   75
incipit effari mediaque in voce resistit;
nunc eadem labente die convivia quaerit,
Iliacosque iterum demens audire labores
exposcit pendetque iterum narrantis ab ore.
post ubi digressi, lumenque obscura vicissim   80
luna premit suadentque cadentia sidera somnos,
sola domo maeret vacua stratisque relictis
incubat. illum absens absentem auditque videtque,

conicere shoot
cerva, f. deer
sagitta, f. arrow
qualis cerva, sagittā coniectā, (furens vagatur)
70 procul from a distance
incautus taken off guard
nemus, n. grove
Crēsius Cretan
fīgere hit
quam... incautam... fixit pastor
agēns tēlīs pursuing with his weapons, *lit.* driving with his weapons
linquere leave, leave implanted
volātilis winged
ferrum, n. steel, blade
illa (cerva) fugā...
silva, f. wood
saltus, m. thicket
peragrāre roam through
Dictaeus of Mount Dicte in Crete
latus, n. side
lētālis deadly
harundō, f. cane, shaft
media... per moenia through the middle of the walled city, *lit.* through the
    middle walls
75 Sīdonius from Sidon
ostentāre show
mediā...in vōce in mid-sentence, *lit.* in mid-voice
resistere stop, stop short
lābī slip away
convīvium, n. banquet
eadem... convivia
Īliacōs...labōrēs the sufferings at Troy
exposcere demand
pendet...nārrantis ab ōre hangs on his words as he tells his story, *lit.* hangs
    from the mouth of him telling the story
80 post afterwards
dīgressī (sunt): dīgredī part
lūmen, n. light
obscūrus darkened, dim, pale
vicissim in turn
premere press, hide
cadere fall, set (of stars)
sīdus, n. star
maerēre grieve
strāta, n.pl. coverings, *here* = couch
incubāre lie on

9

aut gremio Ascanium genitoris imagine capta
detinet, infandum si fallere possit amorem.   85
non coeptae adsurgunt turres, non arma iuventus
exercet portusve aut propugnacula bello
tuta parant: pendent opera interrupta minaeque
murorum ingentes aequataque machina caelo.

Now as soon as Juppiter's consort perceived that Dido was mad
With love and quite beyond caring about her reputation,
She, Juno, approached Venus, making these overtures:-
    A praiseworthy feat, I must say, a fine achievement you've brought
        off,
You and your boy; it should make a great, a lasting name for you –
One woman mastered by the arts of two immortals!
It has not entirely escaped me that you were afraid of my city
And keenly suspicious of towering Carthage's hospitality.
But how will it all end? Where is our rivalry taking us?
Would it not be far better, by arranging a marriage, to seal
A lasting peace? You have got the thing you had set your heart on:
Dido's afire with love, wholly infatuated.
Well then, let us unite these nations and rule them with equal
Authority. Let Dido slave for a Trojan husband,
And let the Tyrians pass into your hand as her dowry.
    Venus, aware that this was double-talk by which
Juno aimed at basing the future Italian empire
On Africa, countered with these words:-
                        Senseless indeed to reject
Such terms and prefer to settle the matter with you by hostilities,
Provided fortune favour the plan which you propose.
But I'm in two minds about destiny, I am not sure if Juppiter
Wishes one city formed of Tyrians and Trojan exiles,
Or would approve a pact or miscegenation between them.
You are his wife: you may ask him to make his policy clearer.
Proceed. I will support you.
                   Queen Juno replied thus:-
    That shall be my task. Now, to solve our immediate problem,
I will briefly put forward a scheme – pray give me your attention.
Aeneas and his unfortunate Dido plan to go
A-hunting in the woods tomorrow, as soon as the sun
Has risen and unshrouded the world below with his rays.

10

gremium, n. lap
Ascanius, m. Ascanius, Aeneas' son
genitōris imāgine capta attracted (*lit.* taken) by his likeness to his father
85 **dētinēre** keep back, hold
īnfandus unutterable
sī...possit to see if she can
adsurgere rise
turris, f. tower
iuventūs, f. youth, young men
portus, m. harbour
prōpugnāculum, n. rampart
bellō tūta to give safety in war
opera, n.pl. building operations
pendēre hang, be suspended
minae...mūrōrum ingentēs the huge threatening walls, *lit.* the huge
    threats of the walls
aequātus level with, reaching to
māchina, f. crane

120 On these two, while the beaters are scurrying about and stopping
The coverts with cordon of nets, I shall pour down a darkling rain-storm
And hail as well, and send thunder hallooing all over the sky.
Dispersing for shelter, the rest of the hunt will be cloaked in the mirk:
But Dido and lord Aeneas, finding their way to the same cave,
Shall meet. I'll be there: and if I may rely on your goodwill,
There I shall join them in lasting marriage, and seal her his,
With Hymen present in person.
                                        Venus made no opposition
To Juno's request, though she smiled at the ingenuity of it.

    Oceanum interea surgens Aurora reliquit.
it portis iubare exorto delecta iuventus,   130
retia rara, plagae, lato venabula ferro,
Massylique ruunt equites et odora canum vis.
reginam thalamo cunctantem ad limina primi
Poenorum exspectant, ostroque insignis et auro
stat sonipes ac frena ferox spumantia mandit.   135
tandem progreditur magna stipante caterva
Sidoniam picto chlamydem circumdata limbo;
cui pharetra ex auro, crines nodantur in aurum,
aurea purpuream subnectit fibula vestem.
nec non et Phrygii comites et laetus Iulus   140
incedunt. ipse ante alios pulcherrimus omnes
infert se socium Aeneas atque agmina iungit.

Ōceanus, m. the Ocean
130 iubar, n. brightness, sun's light
exorīrī rise
dēligere choose
rēte, n. net
rārus scattered, *here* = with a wide mesh
plaga, f. snare
lātus broad
vēnābulum, n. hunting-spear
(*et cum iuventute sunt*) *retia rara...*
Massȳlus African
odōra canum vīs strong, keen-scented dogs, *lit.* the keen-scented strength
   of dogs
cūnctārī delay
ad līmina by the entrance, *lit.* by the thresholds
prīmī, m.pl. nobles, leaders
Poenī, m.pl. the Carthaginians
reginam...cunctantem...primi Poenorum exspectant
ostrum, n. purple
īnsignis splendid
135 sonipēs, m. horse, steed
frēna, n.pl. bit
ferōx fierce, high-spirited
spūmāns foaming
mandere chew, champ
tandem (*Dido*) *progreditur*
stīpāre crowd round
caterva, f. mass of people
pictus painted, *here* = embroidered
chlamys, f. cloak
circumdatus + Form B (accusative) dressed in
limbus, m. border
pharetra, f. quiver
cui (*est*) *pharetra ex auro* (*facta*)
nōdāre knot, tie back
in aurum into a golden clasp
subnectere fasten
fībula, f. brooch
140 nec nōn and also
Phrygius Phrygian, Trojan
Iūlus, m. Ascanius, Aeneas' son
sē īnferre step forward
socius, m. companion
ipse Aeneas pulcherrimus ante alios omnes infert se socium

qualis ubi hibernam Lyciam Xanthique fluenta
deserit ac Delum maternam invisit Apollo
instauratque choros, mixtique altaria circum   145
Cretesque Dryopesque fremunt pictique Agathyrsi;
ipse iugis Cynthi graditur mollique fluentem
fronde premit crinem fingens atque implicat auro,
tela sonant umeris: haud illo segnior ibat
Aeneas, tantum egregio decus enitet ore.   150
postquam altos ventum in montes atque invia lustra,
ecce ferae saxi deiectae vertice caprae
decurrere iugis; alia de parte patentes
transmittunt cursu campos atque agmina cervi
pulverulenta fuga glomerant montesque relinquunt.   155
at puer Ascanius mediis in vallibus acri
gaudet equo iamque hos cursu, iam praeterit illos,

hībernus wintry
Lycia, f. Lycia in southern Asia Minor
Xanthus, m. the river Xanthus in Lycia
fluenta, n.pl. streams, torrent
Dēlos, f. the island of Delos in the Aegean
māternus mother's
invīsere visit
ubi Apollo...deserit ac...invisit
145 **chorus, m.** dance
Crētēs, m.pl. the Cretans
Dryopēs, m.pl. the Dryopes, the people of Epirus in northern Greece
fremere clamour
Agathyrsī, m.pl. the Agathyrsi, a people from Thrace
iugum, n. mountain-ridge
Cynthus, m. Cynthus, a hill on Delos
gradī + Form E (ablative) set foot on
frōns, f. foliage
premere press down, cover
fingere make up, set in place
implicāre entwine
sonāre clash.
haud illō sēgnior no less alertly than he, *lit.* not more sluggish than he
150 **ēgregius** excellent, noble
decus, n. grace
ēnitēre shine out, radiate
ventum (est) they came
invius trackless
lustrum, n. wood
ferus wild
dēicere drive from
vertex, m. summit
capra, f. goat
dēcurrēre = dēcurrērunt: dēcurrere run down
ecce ferae caprae deiectae vertice saxi decurrēre iugis
aliā dē parte elsewhere
patēns open
trānsmittunt cursū they gallop across, *lit.* cross in their running
campus, m. a plain
cervus, m. stag
155 **pulverulentus** dusty
glomerāre crowd together
cervi transmittunt cursu campos patentes atque glomerant agmina
pulverulenta fugā
vallis, f. valley
ācer keen, eager

spumantemque dari pecora inter inertia votis
optat aprum, aut fulvum descendere monte leonem.
    interea magno misceri murmure caelum   160
incipit, insequitur commixta grandine nimbus,
et Tyrii comites passim et Troiana iuventus
Dardaniusque nepos Veneris diversa per agros
tecta metu petiere; ruunt de montibus amnes.
speluncam Dido dux et Troianus eandem   165
deveniunt. prima et Tellus et pronuba Iuno
dant signum; fulsere ignes et conscius aether
conubiis, summoque ulularunt vertice Nymphae.
ille dies primus leti primusque malorum
causa fuit; neque enim specie famave movetur   170
nec iam furtivum Dido meditatur amorem:
coniugium vocat, hoc praetexit nomine culpam.

    Straight away went Rumour through the great cities of Libya –
Rumour, the swiftest traveller of all the ills on earth,
Thriving on movement, gathering strength as it goes; at the start
A small and cowardly thing, it soon puffs itself up,
And walking upon the ground, buries its head in the cloudbase.
The legend is that, enraged with the gods, Mother Earth produced
This creature, her last child, as a sister to Enceladus
And Coeus – a swift-footed creature, a winged angel of ruin,
A terrible, grotesque monster, each feather upon whose body –
Incredible though it sounds – has a sleepless eye beneath it,
And for every eye she has also a tongue, a voice and a pricked ear.
At night she flits midway between earth and sky, through the gloom
Screeching, and never closes her eyelids in sweet slumber:
By day she is perched like a look-out either upon a roof-top
Or some high turret; so she terrorizes whole cities,
Loud-speaker of truth, hoarder of mischievous falsehood, equally.
This creature was now regaling the people with various scandal
In great glee, announcing fact and fiction indiscriminately:
Item, Aeneas has come here, a prince of Trojan blood,
And the beauteous Dido deigns to have her name linked with his;
The couple are spending the winter in debauchery, the whole long
Winter, forgetting their kingdoms, rapt in a trance of lust.

16

pecus, n. herd
iners idle, harmless
aper, m. boar
optat votis aprum spumantem dari
fulvus yellow, tawny
160 miscēre mix, throw into turmoil
īnsequī follow
grandō, f. hail
nimbus, m. rain
Tyrius from Tyre, Phoenician
passim in all directions
Dardanius...nepōs Veneris Venus' Trojan grandson, i.e. Ascanius
dīversus scattered
tēctum, n. house, shelter, *lit.* roof
petiēre = petīvērunt
amnis, m. river
165 spēlunca, f. cave
prīma...Tellūs primeval Earth
prōnuba, f. bride's sponsor
fulsēre = fulsērunt: fulgēre shine, flash
cōnscius witnessing
aethēr, m. air, heaven
cōnubium, n. marriage
ululārunt = ululāvērunt: ululāre howl, cry out
Nymphae, f.pl. the Nymphs, demi-goddesses of the wild
lētum, n. death, doom
malum, n. evil, trouble
170 speciēs, f. outward appearance
fāma, f. reputation
fūrtīvus hidden, secret
neque enim Dido...movetur nec iam...meditatur
coniugium, n. marriage
hōc...nōmine by giving it this name
praetegere conceal
culpa, f. fault, sense of wrong

195   Such gossip did vile Rumour pepper on every mouth.
      Not long before she came to the ears of king Iarbas,
      Whispering inflammatory words and heaping up his resentment.
         He, the son of Ammon by a ravished African nymph,
      Had established a hundred shrines to Jove in his ample realm,
      A hundred altars, and consecrated their quenchless flames
      And vigils unceasing there; the ground was richly steeped in
      Victims' blood, and bouquets of flowers adorned the portals.
      He now, driven out of his mind by that bitter blast of rumour,
      There at the altar, among the presences of the gods,
      Prayed, it is said, to Jove, with importunate, humble entreaty:–
         Almighty Jove, whom now for the first time the Moorish people
      Pledge with wine as they banquet on ornamental couches,
      Do you observe these things? Or are we foolish to shudder
      When you shoot fire, O Father, foolish to be dismayed
      By lightning which is quite aimless and thunder which growls without
           meaning?
      That woman who, wandering within our frontiers, paid to establish
      Her insignificant township, permitted by us to plough up
      A piece of the coast and be queen of it – that woman, rejecting my
           offer
      Of marriage, has taken Aeneas as lord and master there.
      And now that philanderer, with his effeminate following –
      His chin and oil-sleeked hair set off by a Phrygian bonnet –
      That fellow is in possession; while we bring gifts to your shrine.
      If indeed you are there and we do not worship a vain myth.
         Thus did Iarbas pray, with his hands on the altar; and Jove
      Omnipotent, hearing him, bent down his gaze upon Dido's
      City and on those lovers lost to their higher fame.
      Then he addressed Mercury, entrusting to him this errand:–
         Go quick, my son, whistle up the Zephyrs and wing your way
      Down to the Trojan leader, who is dallying now in Carthage
      Without one thought for the city which fate has assigned to be his.
      Carry my dictate along the hastening winds and tell him,
      Not for such ways did his matchless mother guarantee him
      To us, nor for such ends rescue him twice from the Greeks;
      Rather, that he should rule an Italy fertile in leadership
      And loud with war, should hand on a line which sprang from the
           noble
      Teucer and bring the whole world under a system of law.
      If the glory of such great exploits no longer fires his heart
      And for his own renown he will make no effort at all,

234 Does he grudge his son, Ascanius, the glory of Rome to be?
What aim, what hope does he cherish, delaying there in a hostile
Land, with no thought for posterity or his Italian kingdom?
Let him sail. That is the gist. Give him that message from me.
    Jove spake. Mercury now got ready to obey
His father's command. So first he bound on his feet the sandals,
The golden sandals whose wings waft him aloft over sea
And land alike with the hurrying breath of the breezes. Then
He took up his magic wand (with this he summons wan ghosts
From Orcus and consigns others to dreary Tartarus,
Gives sleep or takes it away, seals up the eyes of dead men).
Now, with that trusty wand, he drove the winds and threshed through
The cloud-wrack; descried as he flew the peak and precipitous flanks of
Atlas, that dour mountain which props the sky with his summit –
Atlas, his pine-bristled head for ever enwrapped in a bandeau
Of glooming cloud, for ever beaten by wind and rain;
Snow lies deep on his shoulders, and watercourses plunge down
That ancient's chin, while his shaggy beard is stiff with ice.
Here first did Mercury pause, hovering on beautifully-balanced
Wings; then stooped, dived bodily down to the sea below,
Like a bird which along the shore and around the promontories
Goes fishing, flying low, wave-hopping over the water.
Even so did Mercury skim between earth and sky
Towards the Libyan coast, cutting his path through the winds,
On his way from that mountain giant, Atlas, his mother's sire.

ut primum alatis tetigit magalia plantis,
Aenean fundantem arces ac tecta novantem   260
conspicit. atque illi stellatus iaspide fulva
ensis erat Tyrioque ardebat murice laena
demissa ex umeris, dives quae munera Dido
fecerat, et tenui telas discreverat auro.
continuo invadit: 'tu nunc Karthaginis altae   265
fundamenta locas pulchramque uxorius urbem
exstruis? heu, regni rerumque oblite tuarum!
ipse deum tibi me claro demittit Olympo
regnator, caelum et terras qui numine torquet,
ipse haec ferre iubet celeres mandata per auras: 270
quid struis? aut qua spe Libycis teris otia terris?
si te nulla movet tantarum gloria rerum,
Ascanium surgentem et spes heredis Iuli
respice, cui regnum Italiae Romanaque tellus   275
debetur.' tali Cyllenius ore locutus
mortales visus medio sermone reliquit
et procul in tenuem ex oculis evanuit auram.
    at vero Aeneas aspectu obmutuit amens,
arrectaeque horrore comae et vox faucibus haesit.   280

ut prīmum as soon as
ālātus winged
tetigit: tangere touch, reach
māgālia, n.pl. settlements of huts
planta, f. sole of foot, foot
260 **fundāre** lay the foundation of, establish
arx, f. fortification
tēcta novantem building new houses
stēllātus starred, studded
iaspis, f. jasper
ēnsis, m. sword
mūrex, m. purple dye, purple
laena, f. cloak
dēmissus hanging down
mūnus, n. gift
laena..., munera quae dives Dido...fecerat a cloak..., a gift which
    wealthy Dido had made
tenuis thin, fine
tēla, f. thread
discernere separate out, interweave
265 **continuō** at once
invādere attack, go for
locāre place, lay
uxōrius under a wife's sway
exstruere construct
oblītus + Form D (genitive) forgetting, heedless of
rēgnātor, m. ruler
ipse deum regnator...me demittit
nūmen, n. divine power
torquēre twist, *here* = control
270 **celer** swift
aura, f. breeze
ipse (deum regnator) iubet (me) ferre haec mandata per celeres auras
struere plan
ōtia terere waste time
surgere rise, grow up
275 **respicere** consider
Cyllēnius, m. Mercury, who was born on Mount Cyllene
ōs, n. face, expression, manner
vīsus, m. sight
ēvānēscere vanish
vērō indeed
obmūtēscere be struck dumb
āmēns stupefied
280 **arrēctae (sunt): arrigere** erect, make to rise
coma, f. hair
faucēs, f.pl. throat

21

ardet abire fuga dulcesque relinquere terras,
attonitus tanto monitu imperioque deorum.
heu quid agat? quo nunc reginam ambire furentem
audeat adfatu? quae prima exordia sumat?
atque animum nunc huc celerem nunc dividit illuc   285
in partesque rapit varias perque omnia versat.
haec alternanti potior sententia visa est:
Mnesthea Sergestumque vocat fortemque Serestum,
classem aptent taciti sociosque ad litora cogant,
arma parent et quae rebus sit causa novandis   290
dissimulent; sese interea, quando optima Dido
nesciat et tantos rumpi non speret amores,
temptaturum aditus et quae mollissima fandi
tempora, quis rebus dexter modus. ocius omnes
imperio laeti parent et iussa facessunt.   295
    at regina dolos (quis fallere possit amantem?)
praesensit, motusque excepit prima futuros
omnia tuta timens. eadem impia Fama furenti
detulit armari classem cursumque parari.
saevit inops animi totamque incensa per urbem   300
bacchatur, qualis commotis excita sacris

dulcis sweet, dear
monitus, m. warning
ambīre approach, address
adfātus, m. speech, words
quo...adfatu
exōrdium, n. beginning, approach
sūmere take, adopt
285 **dīvidere** divide, arrange
atque dividit animum celerem nunc huc nunc illuc
versāre turn about
haec alternantī to him as he was considering these alternatives
potior more powerful, better
sententia, f. opinion, plan
Mnēstheus, m.
Sergestus, m. } Trojan nobles, companions of Aeneas
Serestus, m.
classis, f. fleet
aptāre prepare
lītus, n. shore
cōgere bring together
290 **rēbus...novandīs** for renewing action
dissimulāre hide, disguise
quandō since
spērāre hope, expect
aditus, m. approach, way of approach
mollis gentle, kind
fārī speak
dexter right
sese... temptaturum (esse) aditūs et quae (sint)...
ōcius swiftly, *lit.* more swiftly
295 **facessere** carry out
dolus, m. deception
praesentīre have a presentiment of, sense
mōtus, m. movement, preparation
excipere hear, get wind of
impius unholy
Fāma, f. Rumour
dēferre bring news
armāre fit out
cursus, m. journey, voyage
300 **inops animī** at her wits' end, *lit.* with no resources of mind
incēnsus set on fire, furious
bacchārī rave, storm
excitus roused
sacrum, n. holy emblem

23

Thyias, ubi audito stimulant trieterica Baccho
orgia nocturnusque vocat clamore Cithaeron.
tandem his Aenean compellat vocibus ultro:
'dissimulare etiam sperasti, perfide, tantum   305
posse nefas tacitusque mea decedere terra?
nec te noster amor nec te data dextera quondam
nec moritura tenet crudeli funere Dido?
quin etiam hiberno moliris sidere classem
et mediis properas Aquilonibus ire per altum,   310
crudelis? quid, si non arva aliena domosque
ignotas peteres, et Troia antiqua maneret,
Troia per undosum peteretur classibus aequor?
mene fugis? per ego has lacrimas dextramque tuam te
(quando aliud mihi iam miserae nihil ipsa reliqui),   315
per conubia nostra, per inceptos hymenaeos,
si bene quid de te merui, fuit aut tibi quicquam
dulce meum, miserere domus labentis et istam,
oro, si quis adhuc precibus locus, exue mentem.
te propter Libycae gentes Nomadumque tyranni   320
odere, infensi Tyrii; te propter eundem

Thȳias, f. a Maenad, a follower of Bacchus
stimulāre spur on
trietēricus held in alternate years
orgia, n.pl. rites
ubi audito Baccho trieterica orgia (eam) stimulant
Cithaerōn, m. Mount Cithaeron near Thebes
compellāre accuse, challenge
ultrō of one's own accord, *here* = first
305 **perfidus** faithless
nefās, n. crime, wrong
spera(vi)sti, perfide, posse dissimulare etiam...
dēcēdere leave
dextra, f. right hand, pledge
crūdēlis cruel
fūnus, n. death
quĭn etiam moreover, worse still
mōlīrī work to prepare
sīdus, n. star, season
310 **properāre** hurry
Aquilō, m. the North Wind
altum, n. the deep, the sea
quid *here* = tell me
arvum, n. field, territory
aliēnus foreign
ignōtus unknown
undōsus full of waves, surging
aequor, n. sea
ego oro te per has lacrimas...
315 *quando ipsa reliqui nihil aliud mihi iam miserae*
hymenaeus, m. marriage
merēre bene dē + Form E (ablative) deserve well of
(si) tibi quicquam dulce meum fuit if I have been at all dear to you, *lit.*
if anything of mine has been dear to you
miserērī + Form D (genitive) pity
lābī slip away, go to ruin
exuere put off, abandon
mēns, f. mind, intention
et istam... exue mentem
320 **propter + Form B (accusative)** because of
Nomadēs, m.pl. the Nomads, *here* = the Numidians
tyrannus, m. ruler
ōdēre = ōdērunt
īnfēnsus hostile
Libycae gentes Nomadumque tyranni (me) odere, infensi (mihi sunt)
Tyrii

exstinctus pudor et, qua sola sidera adibam,
fama prior. cui me moribundam deseris hospes
(hoc solum nomen quoniam de coniuge restat)?
quid moror? an mea Pygmalion dum moenia frater   325
destruat aut captam ducat Gaetulus Iarbas?
saltem si qua mihi de te suscepta fuisset
ante fugam suboles, si quis mihi parvulus aula
luderet Aeneas, qui te tamen ore referret,
non equidem omnino capta ac deserta viderer.'   330
    dixerat. ille Iovis monitis immota tenebat
lumina et obnixus curam sub corde premebat.
tandem pauca refert: ' ego te, quae plurima fando
enumerare vales, numquam, regina, negabo
promeritam, nec me meminisse pigebit Elissae   335
dum memor ipse mei, dum spiritus hos regit artus.
pro re pauca loquar. neque ego hanc abscondere furto
speravi (ne finge) fugam, nec coniugis umquam
praetendi taedas aut haec in foedera veni.
me si fata meis paterentur ducere vitam   340
auspiciis et sponte mea componere curas,
urbem Troianam primum dulcesque meorum

exstinctus (est) pudor et fama prior, quā solā (ad) sidera adibam

moribundus near to death, ready for death
quoniam since
dē coniuge = **dē coniugis nōmine** from the name of husband
restāre remain
325 **quid moror?** what am I waiting for? *lit.* why am I delaying?
an...dum...? is it until...?
dēstruere destroy
saltem at least
suscepta fuisset: suscipere undertake, conceive
subolēs, f. child
si qua suboles suscepta fuisset mihi de te ante fugam
parvulus dear small
aula, f. hall
referre bring back, recall
330 **capta** *here* = betrayed
monitum, n. command
lūmina, n.pl. eyes
obnīxus struggling, after a struggle
cūram sub corde premēbat he kept stifling his distress in the depths of
    his heart
referre bring back, reply
valēre be well, be able
negāre deny
335 **prōmeritam (esse): prōmerērī** deserve, be deserving
ego numquam negabo te promeritam (esse in illis rebus) quae enumerare
    vales plurima fando I will never deny that you have deserved well of me
    in those matters you can list in words – and there are many of them
mē...pigēbit I shall regret, feel sad
Elissa, f. Elissa, Dido's Phoenician name
dum memor (sum) ipse mei while my memory is still intact, *lit.* while
    I myself am still mindful of myself
spīritus, m. breath, life
regere command, direct
artus, m. limb
prō rē to meet the case, *lit.* for the matter
abscondere conceal
fūrtum, n. secrecy
praetendere hold out, make a pretence of
foedus, n. pledge, obligation
340 **meīs...auspiciīs** on my own terms
patī allow
si fata paterentur me ducere vitam
sponte meā as I would like, *lit.* of my own accord
compōnere settle, calm

reliquias colerem, Priami tecta alta manerent,
et recidiva manu posuissem Pergama victis.
sed nunc Italiam magnam Gryneus Apollo,   345
Italiam Lyciae iussere capessere sortes;
hic amor, haec patria est. si te Karthaginis arces
Phoenissam Libycaeque aspectus detinet urbis,
quae tandem Ausonia Teucros considere terra
invidia est? et nos fas extera quaerere regna.   350
me patris Anchisae, quotiens umentibus umbris
nox operit terras, quotiens astra ignea surgunt,
admonet in somnis et turbida terret imago;
me puer Ascanius capitisque iniuria cari,
quem regno Hesperiae fraudo et fatalibus arvis.   355
nunc etiam interpres divum Iove missus ab ipso
(testor utrumque caput) celeres mandata per auras
detulit: ipse deum manifesto in lumine vidi
intrantem muros vocemque his auribus hausi.
desine meque tuis incendere teque querelis;   360
Italiam non sponte sequor.'

rēliquiae, f.pl. remains, relics
colere care for
recidīvus restored
manū by my own efforts, *lit.* by hand
pōnere place, *here* = found
Pergama, n.pl. Troy
345 **Grȳnēus** Grynean (Apollo was worshipped at Grynium in Lydia)
Lycius belonging to Lycia, Lycian
iussēre = **iussērunt**
capessere make for
sed nunc Gryneus Apollo (iussit me) capessere Italiam
sors, f. lot, oracle
Phoenissus Phoenician
si Karthaginis arces (detinent) te Phoenissam
tandem at length, *here* = tell me
Ausonius Italian
Teucrī, m.pl. the Trojans
350 **invidia, f.** envy, grudge
quae invidia est (tibi)? why do you grudge? *lit.* what grudge do you have?
et nos fas (est) we too are allowed, *lit.* it is right for us too
exterus foreign, abroad
quotiēns whenever
operīre cover
astrum, n. star
igneus fiery
admonēre warn
in somnīs in a dream
turbidus disturbed, unquiet
imāgō, f. likeness, ghost
*quotiens... terras, quotiens... surgunt, turbida imago patris Anchisae
me admonet et terret in somnis*
me (admonet) puer Ascanius
caput, n. head, person
capitis... iniuria cari the wrong I am doing to someone dear to me, *lit.*
the injury of a dear head
355 **Hesperia, f.** the land of the West, Italy
fraudāre cheat
fātālis ordered by fate, destined
interpres, m. intermediary, messenger
testor utrumque caput by your head and mine I swear it, *lit.* I swear by
each of our heads
manifestus clear
haurīre drink, take one's fill of, take in
360 **querēla, f.** complaint
sequī follow, *here* = journey towards

    talia dicentem iamdudum aversa tuetur
huc illuc volvens oculos totumque pererrat
luminibus tacitis et sic accensa profatur:
'nec tibi diva parens generis nec Dardanus auctor,   365
perfide, sed duris genuit te cautibus horrens
Caucasus Hyrcanaeque admorunt ubera tigres.
nam quid dissimulo aut quae me ad maiora reservo?
num fletu ingemuit nostro? num lumina flexit?
num lacrimas victus dedit aut miseratus amantem est?   370
quae quibus anteferam? iam iam nec maxima Iuno
nec Saturnius haec oculis pater aspicit aequis.
nusquam tuta fides. eiectum litore, egentem
excepi et regni demens in parte locavi.
amissam classem, socios a morte reduxi   375
(heu furiis incensa feror!): nunc augur Apollo,
nunc Lyciae sortes, nunc et Iove missus ab ipso
interpres divum fert horrida iussa per auras.
scilicet is superis labor est, ea cura quietos
sollicitat. neque te teneo neque dicta refello: 380
i, sequere Italiam ventis, pete regna per undas.
spero equidem mediis, si quid pia numina possunt,
supplicia hausurum scopulis et nomine Dido
saepe vocaturum. sequar atris ignibus absens

iamdūdum for a long time now, *here* = all the while

tuērī watch

(eum) totum pererrat luminibus tacitis she looks him up and down with eyes which give nothing away, *lit.* she wanders over his whole person with silent eyes

accēnsus kindled, set on fire

profārī speak out

365 **dīva, f.** goddess

Dardanus, m. Dardanus, son of Juppiter and ancestor of the Trojans

auctor, m. originator, ancestor

nec tibi diva (erat) parens nec Dardanus (erat) auctor generis

genuit: gignere bear, give birth to

cautēs, f. crag

horrēns bristling, rough

Hyrcānus Hyrcanian, from Hyrcania near the Caucasus mountains

admōrunt = admōvērunt: admovēre bring towards, thrust at

ūber, n. udder

quae mē ad maiōra reservō? for what greater disasters am I saving myself?

flētus, m. weeping

ingemere groan

flectere bend, turn

370 **victus** overcome, *lit.* conquered

miserārī pity

quae quibus anteferam? what shall I say first? *lit.* what am I to put before what?

Sāturnius…pater the father descended from Saturn, i.e. Juppiter

oculīs…aequīs with a just regard, *lit.* with fair eyes

aspicere look upon

nusquam (est) fides tuta

excepi (eum) eiectum litore

egēre be in need

locāre give a place to

375 **redūcere** lead back, rescue

furia, f. rage

augur, m. prophet

scīlicet no doubt, I suppose

superī, m.pl. the powers above

labor, m. toil, concern

380 **sollicitāre** disturb

ea cura (superos) quietos sollicitat

refellere argue against

pius good, holy, dutiful

supplicium, n. punishment

scopulus, m. rock

spero (te)…supplicia hausurum (esse) et vocaturum (esse)

āter black, dark

31

et, cum frigida mors anima seduxerit artus,   385
omnibus umbra locis adero. dabis, improbe, poenas.
audiam et haec Manes veniet mihi fama sub imos.'
his medium dictis sermonem abrumpit et auras
aegra fugit seque ex oculis avertit et aufert,
linquens multa metu cunctantem et multa parantem   390
dicere. suscipiunt famulae conlapsaque membra
marmoreo referunt thalamo stratisque reponunt.
    at pius Aeneas, quamquam lenire dolentem
solando cupit et dictis avertere curas,
multa gemens magnoque animum labefactus amore   395
iussa tamen divum exsequitur classemque revisit.

Whereupon the Trojans redoubled their efforts, all along
The beach dragging down the tall ships, launching the well-tarred
        bottoms,
Fetching green wood to make oars, and baulks of unfashioned timber
From the forest, so eager they were to be gone.
You could see them on the move, hurrying out of the city.
It looked like an army of ants when, provident for winter,
They're looting a great big corn-heap and storing it up in their own
        house;
Over a field the black file goes, as they carry the loot
On a narrow track through the grass; some are strenuously pushing
The enormous grains of corn with their shoulders, while others marshal
The traffic and keep it moving: their whole road seethes with activity.
Ah, Dido what did you feel when you saw these things going forward?
What moans you gave when, looking forth from your high roof-top,
You beheld the whole length of the beach aswarm with men, and the
        sea's face
Alive with the sound and fury of preparations for sailing!
Excess of love, to what lengths you drive our human hearts!
Once again she was driven to try what tears and entreaties
Could do, and let love beggar her pride – she would leave no appeal
Untried, lest, for want of it, she should all needlessly die.
    Anna, you see the bustle down there on the beach; from all sides
They have assembled; their canvas is stretched to the winds already,
And the elated mariners have garlanded their ships.

385 **frīgidus** icy
   anima, f. soul
   sēdūcere separate
   improbus wicked, vile
   Mānēs, m.pl. the Shades, *here* = the place of the Shades, the Underworld
   abrumpere break off
390 *linquens (eum) multa metu cunctantem* leaving him in frightened hesitation
       about many things, *lit.* leaving him delaying in fear in respect of many
       things
   suscipere undertake, take up
   famula, f. maidservant
   conlāpsa . . . membra . . . referunt they bear her senseless form, *lit.* they bear
       her collapsed limbs
   marmoreus of marble
   repōnere place carefully
   lēnīre soothe
   sōlārī console
395 **animum labefactus** shaken to the heart
   tamen however, *here* = in spite of everything
   exsequī obey, carry out
   revīsere return to

33

419 If I was able to anticipate this deep anguish,
    I shall be able to bear it. But do this one thing, Anna,
    For your poor sister. You were the only confidante
    Of that faithless man: he told you even his secret thoughts:
    You alone know the most tactful way, the best time to approach him.
    Go, sister, and make this appeal to my disdainful enemy:-
    Say that *I* never conspired with the Greeks at Aulis to ruin
    The Trojan people, nor sent squadrons of ships against Troy;
    I never desecrated the ashes of dead Anchises,
    So why must Aeneas be deaf and obdurate to my pleading?
    Why off so fast? Will he grant a last wish to her who unhappily
    Loves him, and wait for a favouring wind, an easier voyage?
    Not for our marriage that was do I plead now – he has forsworn it,
    Nor that he go without his dear Latium and give up his kingdom.
    I ask a mere nothing – just time to give rein to despair and thus calm it,
    To learn from ill luck how to grieve for what I have lost, and to bear it.
    This last favour I beg – oh, pity your sister! – and if he
    Grants it, I will repay him; my death shall be his interest.

      Such were her prayers, and such the tearful entreaties her agonized
Sister conveyed to Aeneas again and again. But unmoved by
Tearful entreaties he was, adamant against all pleadings:
Fate blocked them, heaven stopped his ears lest he turn complaisant.
As when some stalwart oak-tree, some veteran of the Alps,
Is assailed by a wintry wind whose veering gusts tear at it,
Trying to root it up; wildly whistle the branches,
The leaves come flocking down from aloft as the bole is battered;
But the tree stands firm on its crag, for high as its head is carried
Into the sky, so deep do its roots go down towards Hades:
Even thus was the hero belaboured for long with every kind of
Pleading, and his great heart thrilled through and through with the
      pain of it;
Resolute, though, was his mind; unavailingly rolled her tears.

      But hapless Dido, frightened out of her wits by her destiny,
Prayed for death: she would gaze no more on the dome of daylight.
And now, strengthening her resolve to act and to leave this world,
She saw, as she laid gifts on the incense-burning altars –
Horrible to relate – the holy water turn black
And the wine she poured changing uncannily to blood.
She told no one, not even her sister, of this phenomenon.
Again, she had dedicated a chantry of marble within
The palace to her first husband; held it in highest reverence;

34

459 Hung it with snow-white fleeces and with festoons of greenery:
Well, from this shrine, when night covered the earth, she seemed
To be hearing words – the voice of that husband calling upon her.
There was something dirge-like too, in the tones of the owl on the
    roof-top
Whose lonely, repeated cries were drawn out to a long keening.
Besides, she recalled with horror presages, dread forewarnings
Of the prophets of old. Aeneas himself pursued her remorselessly
In dreams, driving her mad; or else she dreamed of unending
Solitude and desertion, of walking alone and eternally
Down a long road, through an empty land, in search of her Tyrians.
Just so does the raving Pentheus see covens of Furies and has the
Delusion of seeing two suns in the sky and a double Thebes:
Just so on the stage does Orestes, the son of Agamemnon,
Move wildly about while his mother pursues him with torches and
    black snakes,
And at the door the avenging Furies cut off his retreat.

    So when, overmastered by grief, she conceived a criminal madness
And doomed herself to death, she worked out the time and method
In secret; then putting on an expression of calm hopefulness
To hide her resolve, she approached her sorrowing sister with these
    words:–
    I have found out a way, Anna – oh, wish me joy of it –
To get him back or else get free of my love for him.
Near Ocean's furthest bound and the sunset is Aethiopia,
The very last place on earth, where giant Atlas pivots
The wheeling sky, embossed with fiery stars, on his shoulders.
I have been in touch with a priestess from there, a Massylian, who
    once,
As warden of the Hesperides' sacred close, was used to
Feed the dragon which guarded their orchard of golden apples,
Sprinkling its food with moist honey and sedative poppy-seeds.
Now this enchantress claims that her spells can liberate
One's heart, or can inject love-pangs, just as she wishes;
Can stop the flow of rivers, send the stars flying backwards,
Conjure ghosts in the night: she can make the earth cry out
Under one's feet, and elm trees come trooping down from the
    mountains.
Dear sister, I solemnly call to witness the gods and you whom
I love, that I do not willingly resort to her magic arts.
You must build up a funeral pyre high in the inner courtyard,

495 And keep it dark: lay on it the arms which that godless man
      Has left on the pegs in our bedroom, all relics of him, and the
            marriage-bed
      That was the ruin of me. To blot out all that reminds me
      Of that vile man is my pleasure and what the enchantress directs.
         So Dido spoke, and fell silent, her face going deadly white.
      Yet Anna never suspected that Dido was planning her own death
      Through these queer rites, nor imagined how frantic a madness
            possessed her,
      Nor feared any worse would happen than when Sychaeus had died.
      So she made the arrangements required of her.
         When in the innermost court of the palace the pyre had been
            built up
      To a great height with pinewood and logs of ilex, the queen
      Festooned the place with garlands and wreathed it with funereal
      Foliage: then she laid on it the clothes, the sword which Aeneas
      Had left, and an effigy of him; she well knew what was to happen.
      Altars were set up all round. Her hair unloosed, the enchantress
      Loudly invoked three hundred deities – Erebus, Chaos,
      Hecate, three in one, and three-faced Diana, the virgin.
      She had sprinkled water which came, she pretended, from Lake Avernus;
      Herbs she had gathered, cut by moonlight with a bronze knife –
      Poisonous herbs all rank with juices of black venom;
      She had found a love charm, a gland torn from the forehead of a
            new-born
      Foal before its mother could get it.
      Dido, the sacramental grain in her purified hands,
      One foot unsandalled, her dress uncinctured, stood by the altars
      Calling upon the gods and the stars that know fate's secrets,
      Death at her heart, and prayed to whatever power it is
      Holds unrequited lovers in its fair, faithful keeping.
         Was night. All over the earth, creatures were plucking the flower
      Of soothing sleep, the woods and the wild seas fallen quiet –
      A time when constellations have reached their mid-career,
      When the countryside is all still, the beasts and the brilliant birds
      That haunt the lakes' wide waters or the tangled undergrowth
      Of the champain, stilled in sleep under the quiet night –
      Cares are lulled and hearts can forget for a while their travails.
      Not so the Phoenician queen: death at her heart, she could not
      Ever relax in sleep, let the night in to her eyes
      Or mind: her agonies mounted, her love reared up again
      And savaged her, till she writhed in a boiling sea of passion.

36

533 So thus she began, her thoughts whirled round in a vicious circle:–
   What shall I do? Shall I, who've been jilted, return to my former
Suitors? go down on my knees for marriage to one of the Nomads
Although, time and again, I once rejected their offers?
Well then, am I to follow the Trojan's fleet and bow to
Their lightest word? I helped them once. Will that help me now?
Dare I think they remember with gratitude my old kindness?
But even if I wished it, who would suffer me, welcome me
Aboard those arrogant ships? They hate me. Ah, duped and ruined! –
Surely by now I should know the ill faith of Laomedon's people?
So then? Shall I sail, by myself, with those exulting mariners,
Or sail against them with all my Tyrian folk about me –
My people, whom once I could hardly persuade to depart from Sidon –
Bidding them man their ships and driving them out to sea again?
Better die – I deserve it – end my pain with the sword.
Sister, you started it all: overborne by my tears, you laid up
These evils to drive me mad, put me at the mercy of a foe.
Oh, that I could have been some child of nature and lived
An innocent life, untouched by marriage and all its troubles!
I have broken the faith I vowed to the memory of Sychaeus.
   Such were the reproaches she could not refrain from uttering.
High on the poop of his ship, resolute now for departure,
Aeneas slept; preparations for sailing were fully completed.
To him in a dream there appeared the shape of the god, returning
Just as he'd looked before, as if giving the same admonitions –
Mercury's very image, the voice, the complexion, the yellow
Hair and the handsome youthful body identical:–
   Goddess-born, can you go on sleeping at such a crisis?
Are you out of your mind, not to see what dangers are brewing up
Around you, and not to hear the favouring breath of the West wind?
Being set upon death, her heart is aswirl with conflicting passions,
Aye, she is brooding now some trick, some desperate deed.
Why are you not going, all speed, while the going is good?
If dawn finds you still here, delaying by these shores,
You'll have the whole sea swarming with hostile ships, there will be
Firebrands coming against you, you'll see this beach ablaze.
Up and away, then! No more lingering! Woman was ever
A veering, weathercock creature.
                              He spoke, and vanished in the darkness.
Then, startled by the shock of the apparition, Aeneas
Snatched himself out of sleep and urgently stirred up his comrades:–
   Jump to it, men! To your watch! Get to the rowing benches!

574 Smartly! Hoist the sails! A god from heaven above
Spurs me to cut the cables, make off and lose not a moment:
This was his second warning. O blessed god, we follow you,
God indeed, and once more we obey the command joyfully!
Be with us! Look kindly upon us! Grant us good sailing weather!
    Thus did Aeneas cry, and flashing his sword from its scabbard,
With the drawn blade he severed the moorings. The same sense of
Urgency fired his comrades all; they cut and ran for it.
The shore lay empty. The ships covered the open sea.
The oarsmen swept the blue and sent the foam flying with hard strokes.

     et iam prima novo spargebat lumine terras
     Tithoni croceum linquens Aurora cubile.   585
     regina e speculis ut primam albescere lucem
     vidit et aequatis classem procedere velis,
     litoraque et vacuos sensit sine remige portus,
     terque quaterque manu pectus percussa decorum
     flaventesque abscissa comas 'pro Iuppiter! ibit   590
     hic,' ait 'et nostris inluserit advena regnis?
     non arma expedient totaque ex urbe sequentur,
     diripientque rates alii navalibus? ite,
     ferte citi flammas, date tela, impellite remos!
     quid loquor? aut ubi sum? quae mentem insania mutat?   595
     infelix Dido, nunc te facta impia tangunt?
     tum decuit, cum sceptra dabas. en dextra fidesque,
     quem secum patrios aiunt portare penates,
     quem subiisse umeris confectum aetate parentem!
     non potui abreptum divellere corpus et undis   600
     spargere? non socios, non ipsum absumere ferro
     Ascanium patriisque epulandum ponere mensis?
     verum anceps pugnae fuerat fortuna. fuisset:
     quem metui moritura? faces in castra tulissem

585 **Tīthōnus, m.** Tithonus, Aurora's husband
    croceus saffron yellow
    cubīle, n. couch, bed
    et iam prima Aurora, linquens Tithoni croceum cubile, spargebat terras...
    specula, f. vantage point
    ut + indicative when
    albēscere begin to dawn
    aequātus level, in line
    vēlum, n. sail
    rēmige: rēmex, m. rower
    (ut) sensit litora (vacua esse) et portus vacuos (esse)
    ter three times
    quater four times
    percussa: percutere strike
    decōrus lovely
590 **flāvēns** golden
    abscindere cut off, tear
    prō Iuppiter! by Juppiter!
    ait she says
    inlūdere + Form C (dative) mock
    advena, m. stranger, foreigner
    non arma (alii) expedient? will some not prepare arms?
    dīripere tear, drag violently
    ratis, f. ship
    nāvālia, n.pl. dockyard
    citus swift
    date tēla hand out weapons
    impellere strike, pull on
    rēmus, m. oar
596 **factum, n.** deed
    tum decuit (impia facta te tangere), cum sceptrum dabas then ought the
        wickedness of your deeds to have come home to you, when you were
        giving him your sceptre
    ēn! see!
    patrius ancestral
    en dextra fidesque (illius) quem...aiunt portare
    subīre undertake, support
    aetās, f. age
600 **abripere** snatch away, carry off
    dīvellere tear apart
    absūmere ferrō murder, *lit.* remove with the sword
    non socios, non ipsum (potui) absumere ferro Ascanium
    epulārī feast upon
    vērum but
    anceps ambiguous, in doubt
    metuere fear
    fax, f. torch

implessemque foros flammis natumque patremque 605
cum genere exstinxem, memet super ipsa dedissem.
Sol, qui terrarum flammis opera omnia lustras,
tuque harum interpres curarum et conscia Iuno,
nocturnisque Hecate triviis ululata per urbes
et Dirae ultrices et di morientis Elissae, 610
accipite haec, meritumque malis advertite numen
et nostras audite preces. si tangere portus
infandum caput ac terris adnare necesse est,
et sic fata Iovis poscunt, hic terminus haeret,
at bello audacis populi vexatus et armis, 615
finibus extorris, complexu avulsus Iuli
auxilium imploret videatque indigna suorum
funera; nec, cum se sub leges pacis iniquae
tradiderit, regno aut optata luce fruatur,
sed cadat ante diem mediaque inhumatus harena. 620
haec precor, hanc vocem extremam cum sanguine fundo.
tum vos, o Tyrii, stirpem et genus omne futurum
exercete odiis, cinerique haec mittite nostro
munera. nullus amor populis nec foedera sunto.
exoriare aliquis nostris ex ossibus ultor 625

605 implēssem = implēvissem
forus, m. gangway
nātus, m. son
exstinxem = exstinxissem: exstinguere extinguish, destroy
mēmet = mē
super above, in addition
memet super ipsa dedissem I indeed (*lit.* myself) would have flung (*lit.*
given) myself on top of all
opus, n. deed, work
interpres, m. agent
nocturnis... Hecatē triviīs ululāta Hecate howled for by night at the
crossroads
610 Dīrae, f.pl. the Furies
ultrix avenging
di morientis Elissae gods who hear Elissa as she is dying, *lit.* gods of
dying Elissa
meritum... malis advertite nūmen turn (to me) the divine regard which
is owed to my wrongs
īnfandus unspeakable, abhorrent
terrīs adnāre make landfalls, *lit.* swim to lands
(*si*) *hic terminus haeret* (if) this is the limit set, *lit.* if this boundary stone
is set firm
616 fīnēs, m.pl. borders, country
extorris + Form E (ablative) exiled from
complexus, m. embrace
āvulsus: āvellere tear from
indignus unworthy, undeserved
lēx, f. law, term (of a treaty)
inīquus unjust, unfair
optātā lūce the days he has longed for, *lit.* the longed-for daylight
fruī + Form E (ablative) enjoy
620 ante diem before his time
inhumātus unburied
harēna, f. sand, desert
hanc vōcem extrēmam these last words, *lit.* this last voice
stirps, f. stock, descendants
exercēte odiis harass with your hatred
cinis, m. ash
mūnus, n. gift, tribute
suntō let there be
625 exoriāre = exoriāris: exorīrī rise up
os, n. bone
ultor, m. avenger
exoriare aliquis... ultor may you, some avenger, rise up

qui face Dardanios ferroque sequare colonos,
nunc, olim, quocumque dabunt se tempore vires.
litora litoribus contraria, fluctibus undas
imprecor, arma armis: pugnent ipsique nepotesque.'
    haec ait, et partes animum versabat in omnes,   630
invisam quaerens quam primum abrumpere lucem.
tum breviter Barcen nutricem adfata Sychaei,
namque suam patria antiqua cinis ater habebat:
' Annam, cara mihi nutrix, huc siste sororem:
dic corpus properet fluviali spargere lympha,   635
et pecudes secum et monstrata piacula ducat.
sic veniat, tuque ipsa pia tege tempora vitta.
sacra Iovi Stygio, quae rite incepta paravi,
perficere est animus finemque imponere curis
Dardaniique rogum capitis permittere flammae.'   640
sic ait. illa gradum studio celebrabat anili.
at trepida et coeptis immanibus effera Dido

sequāre = sequāris
colōnus, m. settler
qui face ferroque sequare colonos Dardanios
ōlim once, *here* = at some time (in the future)
vīrēs, f.pl. power
quocumque dabunt se tempore vires whenever the power presents itself
flūctus, m. wave, breaker
imprecārī pray for
631 invīsus hated, hateful
quam prīmum as soon as possible
invisam quaerens... abrumpere lucem seeking to cut off (*lit.* break off) the
    hateful light of life
breviter briefly
Barcē, f. Barce, Sychaeus' old nurse
nūtrix, f. nurse
adfāta (est): adfārī address
namque for
antīquus ancient, former
suam (nutricem)... cinis ater habebat
sistere place in position, fetch
635 dic... properet tell her to hurry to...
fluviālis of a river
lympha, f. water
mōnstrāre point out, prescribe
piāculum, n. atonement offering
tegere cover
tempora, n.pl. brow
vitta, f. garland
sacra, n.pl. rites, *lit.* sacred things
Stygius of the Underworld
quae rīte incepta parāvi which I have prepared and begun in due fashion,
    lit. which begun in due fashion I have prepared
perficere est animus it is my intention to perform
640 rogus, m. funeral pyre
permittere allow, hand over, commit
gradus, m. step
studium, n. eagerness
celebrāre crowd together, hasten
anīlis of an old woman
trepidus agitated, trembling
coeptum, n. undertaking, intention
immānis frightful, monstrous
efferus savage

43

sanguineam volvens aciem, maculisque trementes
interfusa genas et pallida morte futura,
interiora domus inrumpit limina et altos   645
conscendit furibunda rogos ensemque recludit
Dardanium, non hos quaesitum munus in usus.
hic, postquam Iliacas vestes notumque cubile
conspexit, paulum lacrimis et mente morata
incubuitque toro dixitque novissima verba: 650
'dulces exuviae, dum fata deusque sinebat,
accipite hanc animam meque his exsolvite curis.
vixi et quem dederat cursum Fortuna peregi,
et nunc magna mei sub terras ibit imago.
urbem praeclaram statui, mea moenia vidi,   655
ulta virum poenas inimico a fratre recepi,
felix, heu nimium felix, si litora tantum
numquam Dardaniae tetigissent nostra carinae.'
dixit, et os impressa toro 'moriemur inultae,
sed moriamur' ait. 'sic, sic iuvat ire sub umbras.   660
hauriat hunc oculis ignem crudelis ab alto
Dardanus, et nostrae secum ferat omina mortis.'
dixerat, atque illam media inter talia ferro
conlapsam aspiciunt comites, ensemque cruore
spumantem sparsasque manus. it clamor ad alta   665
atria: concussam bacchatur Fama per urbem.
lamentis gemituque et femineo ululatu
tecta fremunt, resonat magnis plangoribus aether,
non aliter quam si immissis ruat hostibus omnis
Karthago aut antiqua Tyros, flammaeque furentes   670
culmina perque hominum volvantur perque deorum.
audiit exanimis trepidoque exterrita cursu

sanguineus bloodshot
aciēs, f. glance
macula, f. spot
maculis trementes interfusa genas having her quivering cheeks suffused with spots
645 **interiōra domūs...līmina** the inner quarters (*lit.* thresholds) of the palace
inrumpere burst into
cōnscendere climb
furibundus frenzied, in a frenzy
reclūdere unsheathe, draw (a sword)
munus non quaesitum in hos usūs
hīc *here* = then, next
nōtus known, familiar
paulum lacrimīs et mente morāta pausing a moment in tearful thought,
   lit. having paused a little because of tears and thought
650 **torus, m.** couch
novissimus last
exuviae, f.pl. relics
sinere allow
exsolvere release
peragere complete
peregi cursum quem Fortuna dederat
magna mei...imāgō a mighty shade of what I am, *lit.* of me
655 **praeclārus** famous
statuere build, found
poenās recipere exact punishment
fēlīx happy
si...tantum if only
carīna, f. keel
si tantum Dardaniae carinae numquam tetigissent nostra litora
ōs impressa torō having buried her face on the couch
inultus unavenged
660 **iuvat (mē)** it pleases me, I choose
hauriat oculīs crudelis Dardanus hunc ignem ab alto
cruor, m. blood
666 **concutere** shake, shock
gemitus, m. groan
ululātus, m. crying
plangor, m. wailing
nōn aliter quam sī... as it would happen if..., *lit.* not otherwise than if...
immissīs...hostibus when an enemy had invaded
ruere rush, fall, be destroyed
670 **Tyros, f.** Tyre
culmen, n. roof, home
perque culmina hominum perque (culmina) deorum
exanimis distraught
exterritus terror-struck

unguibus ora soror foedans et pectora pugnis
per medios ruit, ac morientem nomine clamat:
'hoc illud, germana, fuit? me fraude petebas?   675
hoc rogus iste mihi, hoc ignes araeque parabant?
quid primum deserta querar? comitemne sororem
sprevisti moriens? eadem me ad fata vocasses,
idem ambas ferro dolor atque eadem hora tulisset.
his etiam struxi manibus patriosque vocavi   680
voce deos, sic te ut posita, crudelis, abessem?
exstinxti te meque, soror, populumque patresque
Sidonios urbemque tuam. date, vulnera lymphis
abluam et, extremus si quis super halitus errat,
ore legam.' sic fata gradus evaserat altos,   685
semianimemque sinu germanam amplexa fovebat
cum gemitu atque atros siccabat veste cruores.
illa graves oculos conata atollere rursus
deficit; infixum stridit sub pectore vulnus.
ter sese attollens cubitoque adnixa levavit,   690
ter revoluta toro est oculisque errantibus alto
quaesivit caelo lucem ingemuitque reperta.
   tum Iuno omnipotens longum miserata dolorem
difficilesque obitus Irim demisit Olympo

46

unguis, m. finger-nail
foedāre disfigure
pugnus, m. fist
soror exanimis audiit trepidoque cursu exterrita per medios ruit, foedans
ora unguibus et pectora pugnis
675 **hoc illud...fuit?** was this what that was?
germāna, f. sister
fraus, f. deceit
me fraude petebas? were you seeking me to deceive me? *lit.* with deceit
parāre prepare, *here* = mean
querī complain about
quid primum deserta querar? what is to be my first complaint now that I
have been abandoned by you?
sprēvistī: spernere scorn
mē...vocāssēs you should have summoned me
idem...ferrō dolor the same agony caused by the sword
680 **etiam** also, *here* = moreover
struere plan, build
his etiam manibus struxi (rogum)
sīc...positā lying thus
ut abessem, crudelis, (a) te sic positā
exstīnxtī = exstīnxistī: exstinguere
patrēs, m.pl. nobles
abluere wash
date...abluam let me wash, *lit.* grant it that I may wash
hālitus, m. breath
685 **legere** collect, catch
gradus, m. step, stair
ēvādere *here* = climb
sēmianimis half-conscious
sinū in her arms
amplectī embrace
fovēre cherish, hold close
siccāre dry
attollere raise
dēficere faint
strīdere hiss, sigh
690 **cubitum, n.** elbow
adnītī rest upon
levāre lift up
revolvī roll back
repertā (luce)
obitus, m. death, end
Īris, f. the goddess Iris

47

quae luctantem animam nexosque resolveret artus.   695
nam quia nec fato merita nec morte peribat,
sed misera ante diem subitoque accensa furore,
nondum illi flavum Proserpina vertice crinem
abstulerat Stygioque caput damnaverat Orco.
ergo Iris croceis per caelum roscida pennis   700
mille trahens varios adverso sole colores
devolat et supra caput astitit. 'hunc ego Diti
sacrum iussa fero teque isto corpore solvo':
sic ait et dextra crinem secat, omnis et una
dilapsus calor atque in ventos vita recessit.   705

695 **luctārī** struggle

nexus tightly-locked

nec fato nec merita morte...

subitus sudden

furor, m. madness

flāvus yellow, fair

Prōserpina, f. Proserpina, goddess of death

vertex, m. summit, top of the head

crīnis, m. lock of hair

damnāre condemn, devote

Orcus, m. Orcus, god of the Underworld

700 **ergō** therefore

croceīs...rōscida pennīs with dew on her saffron wings

trahere drag, draw after

adversō sōle against the sunlight, *lit.* with the sun opposite

dēvolāre fly down

suprā + Form B (accusative) above

astāre stand

Dīs, m. Dis, god of the Underworld

iussa fero hunc (crinem) sacrum Diti

secāre cut

ūnā at the same time

705 **dīlābī** slip away

calor, m. warmth

recēdere pass away

VOCABULARY

A

ā, ab + Form E (ablative) – by, from
abesse – be away: abest, āfuit,
  (āfutūrus)
abīre – go away: abit, abiit, (abitūrus)
ablātus – *see* auferre
abluere – wash: abluit, abluit
abripere – snatch away, carry off:
  abripit, abripuit, abreptus
abrumpere – break off: abrumpit,
  abrūpit, abruptus
abscindere – cut off, tear: abscindit,
  abscidit, abscissus
abscondere – conceal: abscondit,
  abscondit, absconditus
absēns – absent: absentis
abstulit – *see* auferre
absūmere – remove, destroy: absūmit,
  absūmpsit, absūmptus
ac – and
accēnsus – kindled, set on fire
accipere – receive, accept: accipit,
  accēpit, acceptus
ācer, ācris, ācre – keen, eager
aciēs, aciēī, f. – glance
ad + Form B (accusative) – to,
  towards, near, at
adesse – be present: adest, adfuit,
  (adfutūrus)
adfārī – address: adfātur, adfātus est
adfātus, adfātūs, m. – speech, words
adhūc – still
adigere – drive, force: adigit, adēgit,
  adāctus
adīre – approach, go towards: adit,
  adiit, (aditūrus)
aditus, aditūs, m. – approach, way of
  approach

adloquī – speak to, address: adloquitur,
  adlocūtus est
admonēre – warn: admonet, admonuit,
  admonitus
admovēre – bring towards, thrust at:
  admovet, admōvit, admōtus
adnāre – swim to: adnat, adnāvit
adnītī – rest upon: adnītitur, adnīxus
  est
adsurgere – rise: adsurgit, adsurrēxit
advena, advenae, m. – stranger, foreigner
adversus, adversa, adversum – opposite
advertere – turn to: advertit, advertit,
  adversus
aeger, aegra, aegrum – sick, wretched
Aenēās, Aenēae, m. – Aeneas
aequātus, aequāta, aequātum, – level
  (with), reaching to, in line
aequor, aequoris, n. – sea
aequus, aequa, aequum – fair
aetās, aetātis, f. – age
aethēr, aetheris, m. – heaven
Agathyrsī, Agathyrsōrum, m.pl. – the
  Agathyrsi, a people from Thrace
ager, agrī, m. – field
agere – do, drive: agit, ēgit, āctus
agmen, agminis, n. – column, band
agnōscere – recognise: agnōscit,
  agnōvit, agnitus
ait – he, she says, said
aiunt – they say
ālātus, ālāta, ālātum – winged
albēscere – begin to dawn: albēscit
alere – feed: alit, aluit
aliēnus, aliēna, aliēnum – foreign
aliquis, aliquid – someone, something:
  alicuius

51

aliter – otherwise, in another way
alius, alia, aliud – other, another: alīus
altāria, altārium, n.pl. – altars
alternāre – consider alternatives:
    alternat, alternāvit
altum, altī, n. – the deep, the sea
altus, alta, altum – high, lofty
amāns, amantis, m.f. – lover
ambīre – approach, address: ambit,
    . ambiit
ambō, ambae, ambō – both
āmēns – stupefied: āmentis
āmittere – lose: āmittit, āmīsit,
    āmissus
amnis, amnis, m. – river
amor, amōris, m. – love
amplectī – embrace: amplectitur,
    amplexus est
an – *asks a question*
anceps – ambiguous, in doubt:
    ancipitis
Anchīsēs, Anchīsae, m. – Anchises,
    Aeneas' father
anīlis, anīlis, anīle – of an old woman
anima, animae, f. – soul
animus, animī, m. – mind, heart, resolve,
    intention
Anna, Annae, f. – Anna, Dido's sister
ante + Form B (accusative) – before
anteferre – put before: antefert,
    antetulit, antelātus
antequam – before
antīquus, antīqua, antīquum – ancient,
    former
aper, aprī, m. – boar
Apollō, Apollinis, m. – the god Apollo
aptāre – prepare: aptat, aptāvit, aptātus
Aquilō, Aquilōnis, m. – the North Wind
āra, ārae, f. – altar
ardēre – burn, blaze, be eager: ardent
    arsit, (arsūrus)
arguere – prove, reveal: arguit, arguit,
    argūtus
arma, armōrum, n.pl. – arms
armāre – fit out: armat, armāvit, armātus
arrigere – erect, make to rise: arrigit,
    arrēxit, arrēctus

artus, artūs, m. – limb
arvum, arvī, n. – field, territory
arx, arcis, f. – citadel, fortification
Ascanius, Ascaniī, m. – Ascanius,
    Aeneas' son
aspectus, aspectūs, m. – sight
aspicere – look upon: aspicit, aspexit,
    aspectus
astāre – stand: astat, astitit
astrum, astrī, n. – star
at – but
āter, ātra, ātrum – black, dark
atque – and
ātrium, ātriī, n. – hall
attollere – raise: attollit
attonitus, attonita, attonitum –
    astonished
auctor, auctōris, m. – originator,
    ancestor
audāx – bold, brave: audācis
audēre – dare: audet, ausus est
audīre – hear: audit, audīvit, audītus
auferre – take away: aufert, abstulit,
    ablātus
augur, auguris, m. – prophet
aula, aulae, f. – hall
aura, aurae, f. – breeze
aureus, aurea, aureum – golden
auris, auris, f. – ear
Aurōra, Aurōrae, f. – Aurora, goddess
    of the dawn
aurum, aurī, n. – gold
Ausonius, Ausonia, Ausonium –
    Italian
auspicium, auspiciī, n. – omen,
    authority, terms
aut – or
auxilium, auxiliī, n. – help
āvellere – tear from: āvellit, āvulsit,
    āvulsus
āvertere – turn away: āvertit, āvertit,
    āversus

B

bacchārī – rave, storm: bacchātur,
    bacchātus est
Bacchus, Bacchī, m. – the god Bacchus

Barcē, Barcēs, f. - Barce, Sychaeus' old nurse
bellum, bellī, n. - war
bene - well
bidēns, bidentis, f. - a young sheep
breviter - briefly

C

cadere - fall, set (of stars): cadit, cecidit, (cāsūrus)
caecus, caeca, caecum - blind, hidden
caedēs, caedis, f. - slaughter, murder
caelum, caelī, n. - sky, heaven
calor, calōris, m. - warmth
campus, campī, m. - a plain
candēns - white: candentis
canere - sing, describe: canit, cecinit
canis, canis, m. - dog
capere - take, capture: capit, cēpit, captus
capessere - make for: capessit, capessivit
capra, caprae, f. - goat
caput, capitis, n. - head, person
carina, carinae, f. - keel
carpere - pluck, wear away: carpit, carpsit, carptus
cārus, cāra, cārum - dear
castra, castrōrum, n.pl. - camp
caterva, catervae, f. - crowd, mass of people
Caucasus, Caucasī, m. - the Caucasian mountains
causa, causae, f. - cause, reason
cautēs, cautis, f. - crag
celebrāre - crowd together, hasten: celebrat, celebrāvit, celebrātus
celer, celeris, celere - swift
Cerēs, Cereris, f. - the goddess Ceres
cerva, cervae, f. - deer
cervus, cervī, m. - stag
chlamys, chlamydis, f. - cloak
chorus, chorī, m. - dance
cinis, cineris, m. - ash
circum + Form B (accusative) - around

circumdatus, circumdata, circumdatum + Form B (accusative) - dressed in
Cithaerōn, Cithaerōnis, m. - Mount Cithaeron near Thebes
citus, cita, citum - swift
clāmāre - shout: clāmat, clāmāvit
clāmor, clāmōris, m. - cry, shout
clārus, clāra, clārum - clear
classis, classis, f. - fleet
coepisse - have begun: coepit, coeptus
coeptum, coeptī, n. - undertaking, intention
cōgere - bring together: cōgit, coēgit, coāctus
colere - care for: colit, coluit, cultus
colōnus, colōnī, m. - settler
color, colōris, m. - colour
coma, comae, f. - hair
comes, comitis, m. - companion
commiscēre - mingle: commiscet, commiscuit, commixtus
commovēre - shake, brandish: commovet, commōvit, commōtus
compellāre - accuse, challenge: compellat, compellāvit, compellātus
complexus, complexūs, m. - embrace
compōnere - settle, calm: compōnit, composuit, compositus
cōnārī - try: cōnātur, cōnātus est
concutere - shake, shock: concutit, concussit, concussus
cōnficere - wear out: cōnficit, cōnfēcit, cōnfectus
conicere - shoot: conicit, coniēcit, coniectus
coniugium, coniugiī, n. - marriage
coniūnx, coniugis, m.f. - husband, wife
conlābī - collapse: conlābitur, conlāpsus est
cōnscendere - climb: cōnscendit, cōnscendit
cōnscius, cōnscia, cōnscium - witnessing
cōnsīdere - settle: cōnsīdit, cōnsēdit, cōnsessus
cōnspicere - catch sight of: cōnspicit, cōnspexit, cōnspectus

53

cōnsulere – consult, examine: cōnsulit,
cōnsuluit, cōnsultus
continuō – at once
contrārius, contrāria, contrārium –
opposing
cōnubium, cōnubiī, n. – marriage
convīvium, convīviī, n. – banquet
cor, cordis, n. – heart
cornū, cornūs, n. – horn
corpus, corporis, n. – body
crēdere – believe: crēdit, crēdidit,
crēditus
Crēsius, Crēsia, Crēsium – Cretan
Crētēs, Crētum, m.pl. – the Cretans
crīnis, crīnis, m. – hair, lock of hair
croceus, crocea, croceum – saffron
yellow
crūdēlis, crūdēlis, crūdēle – cruel
cruor, cruōris, m. – blood
cubīle, cubīlis, n. – couch, bed
cubitum, cubitī, n. – elbow
culmen, culminis, n. – roof, home
culpa, culpae, f. – fault, source of
temptation, sense of wrong
cum – when
cum + Form E (ablative) – with
cūnctārī – delay: cūnctātur, cūnctātus
est
cupere – desire: cupit, cupīvit
cūra, cūrae, f. – concern, distress,
passion, responsibility, anxiety
cursus, cursūs, m. – journey, voyage,
course, running
Cyllēnius, Cyllēniī, m. – Mercury,
who was born on Mount Cyllene
Cynthus, Cynthī, m. – Cynthus, a hill
on Delos

D
damnāre – condemn, devote: damnat,
damnāvit, damnātus
Dardanius, Dardania, Dardanium –
Trojan
Dardanus, Dardanī, m. – Dardanus,
founder of the Trojan race, a
Trojan

dare – give, grant, hand out: dat,
dedit, datus
sē dare – present oneself
dē + Form E (ablative) – according to,
about, from
dēbēre – owe: dēbet, dēbuit, dēbitus
dēcēdere – leave: dēcēdit, dēcessit,
(dēcessūrus)
dēceptus, dēcepta, dēceptum – cheated,
bereaved
decēre – be fitting: decet, decuit
decōrus, decōra, decōrum – lovely
dēcurrere – run down: dēcurrit,
dēcurrit
decus, decoris, n. – grace
dēferre – bring, bring news: dēfert,
dētulit, dēlātus
dēficere – fail, faint: dēficit, dēfēcit
dēgener, dēgeneris, dēgenere – ignoble,
inferior
dēhīscere – gape open: dēhīscit
dēicere – drive from: dēicit, dēiēcit,
dēiectus
dēligere – choose: dēligit, dēlēgit,
dēlēctus
Dēlos, Dēlī, f. – the island of Delos in
the Aegean
dēlūbrum, dēlūbrī, n. – shrine
dēmēns – mad: dēmentis
dēmittere – send down: dēmittit,
dēmīsit, dēmissus
dēmissus, dēmissa, dēmissum –
hanging down
dēscendere – come down: dēscendit,
dēscendit, (dēscēnsūrus)
dēserere – abandon: dēserit, dēseruit,
dēsertus
dēsinere – stop: dēsinit, dēsiit
dēstruere – destroy: dēstruit, dēstrūxit,
dēstrūctus
dētinēre – keep back, hold: dētinet,
dētinuit, dētentus
deus, deī, m. – god
dēvenīre – go down into: dēvenit,
dēvēnit, (dēventūrus)
dēvolāre – fly down: dēvolat, dēvolāvit

54

dexter, dextra, dextrum – right
  dextera, dexterae, f. – right hand
  dextra, dextrae, f. – right hand
dī – *see* deus
dīcere – say, speak, tell: dīcit, dīxit,
  dictus
Dictaeus, Dictaea, Dictaeum – of
  Mount Dicte in Crete
dictum, dictī, n. – word
Dīdō, Dīdōnis, f. – Dido
diēs, diēī, m.f. – day
difficilis, difficilis, difficile – difficult
dīgredī – part: dīgreditur, dīgressus est
dīlābī – slip away: dīlābitur, dīlāpsus est
dīmovēre – move aside, dispel: dīmovet,
  dīmōvit, dīmōtus
Dīrae, Dīrārum, f.pl. – the Furies
dīripere – tear, drag violently: dīripit,
  dīripuit, dīreptus
Dīs, Dītis, m. – Dis, god of the Underworld
discernere – separate out, interweave:
  discernit, discrēvit, discrētus
dissimulāre – hide, disguise, pretend:
  dissimulat, dissimulāvit, dissimulātus
dīva, dīvae, f. – goddess
dīvellere – tear apart: dīvellit, dīvellit,
  dīvulsus
dīversus, dīversa, dīversum – scattered
dīves – rich, wealthy: dīvitis
dīvidere – divide, arrange: dīvidit, dīvīsit,
  dīvīsus
dīvus, dīvī, m. – god
dolēre – grieve: dolet, doluit
dolor, dolōris, m. – grief, pain, agony
dolus, dolī, m. – trick, deception
domus, domūs, f. – house, palace
dōnum, dōnī, n. – gift
Dryopēs, Dryopum, m.pl. – the Dryopes,
  the people of Epirus in northern
  Greece
dubius, dubia, dubium – uncertain,
  wavering
dūcere – lead, bring: dūcit, dūxit, ductus
dulcis, dulcis, dulce – sweet, dear
dum + subjunctive – until

dum + indicative – while
dūrus, dūra, dūrum – hard, harsh
dux, ducis, m. – leader

E

ē, ex + Form E (ablative) – out of, from
ecce! – see!
effārī – speak out, reveal one's thoughts:
  effātur, effātus est
efferus, effera, efferum – savage
egēre – be in need: eget, eguit
ego, meī – I
ēgregius, ēgregia, ēgregium – excellent,
  noble
ēheu – alas
ēicere – cast up, wreck: ēicit, ēiēcit,
  ēiectus
Elissa, Elissae, f. – Elissa, Dido's
  Phoenician name
ēn! – see!
enim – for
ēnitēre – shine out, radiate: ēnitet,
  ēnituit
ēnsis, ēnsis, m. – sword
ēnumerāre – list: ēnumerat, ēnumerāvit,
  ēnumerātus
epulārī – feast upon: epulātur, epulātus
  est
eques, equitis, m. – horseman
equidem – indeed
equus, equī, m. – horse
Erebus, Erebī, m. – the Underworld
ergō – therefore
errāre – wander: errat, errāvit
esse – be: est, fuit, (futūrus)
ēsse – eat: ēst, ēdit, ēsus
et – and, too
etiam – even, also
  quīn etiam – moreover, worse still
ēvādere – go out, up: ēvādit, ēvāsit,
  (ēvāsūrus)
ēvānēscere – vanish: ēvānēscit,
  ēvānuit
ex, ē + Form E (ablative) – out of,
  from

exanimis, exanimis, exanime –
  distraught
excipere – hear, get wind of, receive:
  excipit, excēpit, exceptus
excitus, excita, excitum – roused
exercēre – practise, harass: exercet,
  exercuit, exercitus
exhaustus, exhausta, exhaustum –
  drained to the dregs, seen through
  to the end
exōrdium, exōrdiī, n. – beginning,
  approach
exorīrī – rise (up): exoritur, exortus est
expedīre – prepare: expedit, expedīvit,
  expedītus
exposcere – demand: exposcit,
  expoposcit
exquīrere – seek: exquīrit, exquīsīvit,
  exquīsītus
exsequī – obey, carry out: exsequitur,
  exsecūtus est
exsolvere – release: exsolvit, exsolvit,
  exsolūtus
exspectāre – wait for: exspectat,
  exspectāvit, exspectātus
exstinguere – extinguish, destroy:
  exstinguit, exstīnxit, exstīnctus
exstruere – construct: exstruit,
  exstrūxit, exstrūctus
exta, extōrum, n.pl. – entrails
exterritus, exterrita, exterritum –
  terror-struck
exterus, extera, exterum – foreign,
  abroad
extorris, extorris, extorre + Form E
  (ablative) – exiled from
extrēmus, extrēma, extrēmum – last
exuere – put off, abandon: exuit,
  exuit, exūtus
exuviae, exuviārum, f.pl. – relics

F
facere – do, make: facit, fēcit, factus
facessere – carry out: facessit,
  facessīvit, facessītus
factum, factī, n. – deed

fallere – cheat, betray: fallit, fefellit,
  falsus
fāma, fāmae, f. – reputation, rumour
famula, famulae, f. – maidservant
fandī, fandō – see fārī
fārī – speak: fātur, fātus est
fās, n. – right
fātālis, fātālis, fātāle – ordered by
  fate, destined
fatērī – confess: fatētur, fassus est
fātum, fātī, n. – fate, death
faucēs, faucium, f.pl. – throat
fax, facis, f. – torch
fēlix – happy: fēlīcis
fēmineus, fēminea, fēmineum – of
  women
ferōx – fierce, high-spirited: ferōcis
ferre – bring, carry, bear: fert, tulit,
  lātus
  sē ferre – bear oneself
ferrum, ferrī, n. – steel, sword,
  blade
ferus, fera, ferum – wild
fībula, fībulae, f. – brooch
fidēs, fideī, f. – belief, trust
fīgere – hit: fīgit, fīxit, fīxus
fingere – make up, set in place,
  imagine: fingit, fīnxit, fictus
fīnis, fīnis, m. – end
  pl. borders, country
fīxus, fīxa, fīxum – fixed
flamma, flammae, f. – flame, passion
flammāre – inflame, burn: flammat,
  flammāvit, flammātus
flāvēns – golden: flāventis
flāvus, flāva, flāvum – yellow, fair
flectere – bend, turn: flectit, flexit,
  flexus
flētus, flētūs, m. – weeping
flūctus, flūctūs, m. – wave, breaker
fluenta, fluentōrum, n.pl. – streams,
  torrent
fluere – flow: fluit, flūxit
fluviālis, fluviālis, fluviāle – of a river
foedāre – disfigure: foedat, foedāvit,
  foedātus

56

foedus, foederis, n. – pledge, obligation, treaty
forsan – perhaps
fortis, fortis, forte – brave
fortūna, fortūnae, f. – luck, fortune
forus, forī, m. – gangway
fovēre – cherish, hold close: fovet, fōvit
frāter, frātris, m. – brother
frāternus, frāterna, frāternum – of a brother, of a relation
fraudāre – cheat: fraudat, fraudāvit, fraudātus
fraus, fraudis, f. – deceit
fremere – clamour, resound: fremit, fremuit
frēna, frēnōrum, n.pl. – bit
frīgidus, frīgida, frīgidum – icy
frōns, frondis, f. – foliage
fruī + Form E (ablative) – enjoy: fruitur, frūctus est
fuga, fugae, f. – flight, departure
fugere – run away: fugit, fūgit, (fugitūrus)
fulgēre – shine, flash: fulget, fulsit
fulmen, fulminis, n. – thunderbolt
fulvus, fulva, fulvum – yellow, tawny
fundāmentum, fundāmentī, n. – foundation
fundāre – lay the foundation of, establish: fundat, fundāvit, fundātus
fundere – pour (an offering), pour out: fundit, fūdit, fūsus
fūnus, fūneris, n. – death
furēns – mad, enraged, raging: furentis
furia, furiae, f. – rage
furibundus, furibunda, furibundum – frenzied, in a frenzy
furor, furōris, m. – madness
fūrtīvus, fūrtīva, fūrtīvum – hidden, secret
fūrtum, fūrtī, n. – secrecy

G

Gaetūlus, Gaetūla, Gaetūlum – of the Gaetuli, a tribe in North Africa
gaudēre + Form E (ablative) – rejoice: gaudet, gāvīsus est
gemere – groan: gemit, gemuit
gemitus, gemitūs, m. – groan
gena, genae, f. – cheek
genitor, genitōris, m. – father
gēns, gentis, f. – family, tribe
genus, generis, n. – race, descent
germāna, germānae, f. – sister
gignere – bear, give birth to: gignit, genuit, genitus
glomerāre – crowd together: glomerat, glomerāvit, glomerātus
glōria, glōriae, f. – glory
gradī + Form E (ablative) – set foot on: graditur, gressus est
gradus, gradūs, m. – step, stair
grandō, grandinis, f. – hail
gravis, gravis, grave – heavy, deep, serious
gremium, gremiī, n. – lap
Grȳnēus, Grȳnēa, Grȳnēum – Grynean, belonging to Grynium in Lydia

H

habēre – have, keep: habet, habuit, habitus
haerēre – stick, be set firm: haeret, haesit
hālitus, hālitūs, m. – breath
harēna, harēnae, f. – sand, desert
harundō, harundinis, f. – cane, shaft
haud – not
haurīre – drink, take one's fill of, take in: haurit, hausit, haustus
Hecatē, Hecatēs, f. – the goddess Hecate
hērēs, hērēdis, m. – heir
Hesperia, Hesperiae, f. – the land of the West, Italy
heu = ēheu
hībernus, hīberna, hībernum – wintry, in the winter

hic, haec, hoc – this: huius
hīc – here, then
homō, hominis, m. – man
honōs, honōris, m. – honour
hōra, hōrae, f. – hour
horrēns – bristling, rough: horrentis
horridus, horrida, horridum –
    loathsome, horrible
horror, horrōris, m. – horror
hospes, hospitis, m. – guest
hostis, hostis, m. – enemy
hūc – here, to here
hūc...illūc – here and there
hymenaeus, hymenaeī, m. – marriage
Hyrcānus, Hyrcāna, Hyrcānum –
    Hyrcanian, from Hyrcania near
    the Caucasus mountains

I
iactāre – toss, buffet: iactat, iactāvit,
    iactātus
iam – now, at present
    iam...iam – sometimes...some-
    times
iamdūdum – for a long time now
Iarbas, Iarbae, m. – Iarbas, king of
    the Gaetuli
iaspis, iaspidis, f. – jasper
īdem, eadem, idem – the same: eiusdem
ignārus, ignāra, ignārum – unknowing,
    ignorant
igneus, ignea, igneum – fiery
ignis, ignis, m. – fire, flame
    pl. lightning
ignōtus, ignōta, ignōtum – unknown
Īliacus, Īliaca, Īliacum – Trojan, at Troy
ille, illa, illud – he, she, it, that: illīus
illūc – there
imāgō, imāginis, f. – likeness, ghost,
    shade
immānis, immānis, immāne – frightful,
    monstrous
immittere – send in: immittit, immīsit,
    immissus
immōtus, immōta, immōtum – unshake-
    able, motionless

impellere – strike, make an impression
    on, pull on: impellit, impulit,
    impulsus
impēnsus, impēnsa, impēnsum – heavy,
    great
imperium, imperiī, n. – command
impius, impia, impium – unholy,
    wicked
implēre – fill: implet, implēvit,
    implētus
implicāre – entwine: implicat,
    implicuit, implicitus
implōrāre – beg: implōrat, implōrāvit,
    implōrātus
impōnere – put (on): impōnit, imposuit,
    impositus
imprecārī – pray for: imprecātur,
    imprecātus est
imprimere – press upon: imprimit,
    impressit, impressus
improbus, improba, improbum –
    wicked, vile
īmus, īma, īmum – lowest
in + Form B (accusative) – into, for
    + Form E (ablative) – in, on
incautus, incauta, incautum – taken
    off guard
incēdere – go along: incēdit, incessit
incendere – burn, set on fire: incendit,
    incendit, incēnsus
incēnsus, incēnsa, incēnsum – set
    on fire, furious
incipere – begin: incipit, incēpit,
    inceptus
incubāre – lie on: incubat, incubuit
indignus, indigna, indignum – unworthy,
    undeserved
iners – idle, harmless: inertis
īnfandus, īnfanda, īnfandum – un-
    utterable, unspeakable,
    abhorrent
īnfēlīx – unhappy, wretched: īnfēlīcis
īnfēnsus, īnfēnsa, īnfēnsum – hostile
īnferre – bring in: īnfert, intulit,
    inlātus
sē īnferre – step forward

58

infīxus, infīxa, infīxum – fastened in, implanted
inflectere – bend, alter: inflectit, inflexit, inflexus
ingemere – groan: ingemit, ingemuit
ingēns – huge: ingentis
inhiāre – peer into: inhiat, inhiāvit
inhumātus, inhumāta, inhumātum – unburied
inimīcus, inimīca, inimīcum – hostile
inīquus, inīqua, inīquum – unjust, unfair
iniūria, iniūriae, f. – wrong
inlūdere + Form C (dative) – mock: inlūdit, inlūsit
inops – helpless, with no resources: inopis
inrumpere – burst into: inrumpit, inrūpit, inruptus
insānia, insāniae, f. – madness
insequī – follow: insequitur, insecūtus est
insignis, insignis, insigne – splendid
insomnium, insomniī, n. – dream
instaurāre – begin a ceremony again, renew: instaurat, instaurāvit, instaurātus
inter + Form B (accusative) – between
intereā – meanwhile
interfūsus, interfūsa, interfūsum – suffused
interior, interior, interius – inner
interpres, interpretis, m. – intermediary, messenger, agent
interruptus, interrupta, interruptum – interrupted, broken off
intrāre – enter: intrat, intrāvit
inultus, inulta, inultum – unavenged
invādere – attack, go for: invādit, invāsit, (invāsūrus)
invidia, invidiae, f. – envy, grudge
invīsere – visit: invīsit, invīsit, invīsus
invīsus, invīsa, invīsum – hated, hateful
invius, invia, invium – trackless
Iovis – see Iuppiter
ipse, ipsa, ipsum – himself, herself, oneself: ipsīus

īre – go: it, iit, (itūrus)
Iris, Iris, f. – the goddess Iris
is, ea, id – he, she, it: eius
iste, ista, istud – that: istīus
Italia, Italiae, f. – Italy
iterum – again
iubar, iubaris, n. – brightness, sun's light
iubēre – order: iubet, iussit, iussus
iugālis, iugālis, iugāle – of marriage
iugum, iugī, n. – mountain-ridge
Iūlus, Iūlī, m. – Ascanius, Aeneas' son
iungere – join: iungit, iūnxit, iūnctus
Iūnō, Iūnōnis, f. – the goddess Juno
Iuppiter, Iovis, m. – the god Juppiter
iūs, iūris, n. – law
iussum, iussī, n. – command
iuvāre – help: iuvat, iūvit, (iuvātūrus)
iuvat mē – it pleases me, I choose
iuventūs, iuventūtis, f. – youth, young men

K
Karthāgō, Karthāginis, f. – Carthage

L
labāre – totter, waver: labat, labāvit
labefacere – shake: labefacit, labefēcit, labefactus
lābī – slip away, go to ruin: lābitur, lāpsus est
labor, labōris, m. – toil, suffering, concern
lacrima, lacrimae, f. – tear
laena, laenae, f. – cloak
laetus, laeta, laetum – glad, happy
lāmentum, lāmentī, n. – lament
lampas, lampadis, f. – torch
latus, lateris, n. – side
lātus, lāta, lātum – broad
lātus – see ferre
lēctus, lēcta, lēctum – chosen
legere – collect, catch: legit, lēgit, lēctus
lēgifer, lēgifera, lēgiferum – law-giving
lēnīre – soothe: lēnit, lēnīvit
leō, leōnis, m. – lion

59

letalis, letalis, letale – deadly
letum, leti, n. – death, doom
levare – lift up: levat, levavit
lex, legis, f. – law, term (of a treaty)
Libycus, Libyca, Libycum – Libyan,
    African
limbus, limbi, m. – border
limen, liminis, n. – threshold
linquere – leave: linquit, liquit
litus, litoris, n. – shore
locare – place, lay, give a place to:
    locat, locavit, locatus
locus, loci, m. – place
longus, longa, longum – long
loqui – speak: loquitur, locutus est
luctari – struggle: luctatur, luctatus
    est
ludere – play: ludit, lusit, lusus
lumen, luminis, n. – light
    pl. eyes
luna, lunae, f. – moon
lustrare – purify, range over: lustrat,
    lustravit, lustratus
lustrum, lustri, n. – wood
lux, lucis, f. – light, daylight
Lyaeus, Lyaei, m. – the Deliverer, i.e.
    the god Bacchus
Lycia, Lyciae, f. – Lycia in southern
    Asia Minor
Lycius, Lycia, Lycium – belonging
    to Lycia, Lycian
lympha, lymphae, f. – water

M
machina, machinae, f. – crane
mactare – sacrifice: mactat, mactavit,
    mactatus
macula, maculae, f. – spot
maerere – grieve: maeret, maeruit
magalia, magalium, n.pl. – settlements
    of huts
magnus, magna, magnum – big, great,
    mighty
    maior, maior, maius – greater
    maximus, maxima, maximum –
        greatest

male – not, scarcely
malum, mali, n. – evil, trouble, wrong
mandatum, mandati, n. – instruction
mandere – chew, champ: mandit,
    mandit, mansus
manere – remain: manet, mansit,
    (mansurus)
Manes, Manium, m.pl. – the Shades
manifestus, manifesta, manifestum –
    clear
manus, manus, f. – hand
marmoreus, marmorea, marmoreum –
    of marble
Massylus, Massyla, Massylum – African
maternus, materna, maternum –
    mother's
maximus – see magnus
meditari – dwell upon, contemplate:
    meditatur, meditatus est
medius, media, medium – middle,
    mid, central
medulla, medullae, f. – marrow (of
    the bones)
membrum, membri, n. – limb
memet = me
meminisse – remember: meminit
memor + Form D (genitive) – mindful
    of: memoris
mens, mentis, f. – mind, intention,
    thought
mensa, mensae, f. – table
merere – deserve: meret, meruit,
    meritus
merere bene de + Form E (ablative)
    – deserve well of
meritus, merita, meritum –
    deserved, owed
metuere – fear: metuit, metuit
metus, metus, m. – fear
meus, mea, meum – my
mille – a thousand
minae, minarum, f.pl. – threats
miscere – mix, throw into turmoil:
    miscet, miscuit, mixtus
miser, misera, miserum – wretched,
    poor

miserārī – pity: miserātur, miserātus
  est
miserērī + Form D (genitive) – pity:
  miserētur, miseritus est
mittere – send: mittit, mīsit, missus
Mnēstheus, m. – Mnestheus, companion
  of Aeneas
modus, modī, m. – way
moenia, moenium, n.pl. – walls
mōlīrī – work to prepare: mōlītur,
  mōlītus est
mollis, mollis, molle – soft, gentle,
  kind
monitus, monitūs, m. – warning,
  command
mōns, montis, m. – mountain
mōnstrāre – point out, prescribe:
  mōnstrat, mōnstrāvit, mōnstrātus
morārī – delay: morātur, morātus est
morī – die: moritur, mortuus est
  moritūrus, moritūra, moritūrum –
  about to die
moribundus, moribunda, moribundum
  – near to death, ready for death
mors, mortis, f. – death
mortālis, mortālis, mortāle – mortal
mōs, mōris, m. – custom, manner
mōtus, mōtūs, m. – movement,
  preparation
movēre – move: movet, mōvit, mōtus
multus, multa, multum – much, many
  plūrimus, plūrima, plūrimum –
  most, very many
mūnus, mūneris, n. – gift, tribute
mūrex, mūricis, m. – purple dye,
  purple
murmur, murmuris, n. – murmuring
mūrus, mūrī, m. – wall
mūtāre – change, alter: mūtat, mūtāvit,
  mūtātus

N
nam – for
namque – for
nārrāre – tell a story: nārrat, nārrāvit,
  nārrātus

nātus, nātī, m. – son
nāvālia, nāvālium, n.pl. – dockyard
-ne – *asks a question*
nē – lest, in order that...not
nec – nor, and not
  nec...nec – neither...nor
  nec nōn – and also
necesse – necessary
nefās, n. – crime, wrong
negāre – deny: negat, negāvit,
  negātus
nemus, nemoris, n. – grove
nepōs, nepōtis, m. – grandson,
  descendant
neque – neither, nor
nescīre – not know: nescit, nescīvit
nescius, nescia, nescium – not know-
  ing, in ignorance
nexus, nexa, nexum – tightly-locked
nihil – nothing
nimbus, nimbī, m. – rain
nimium – too much, too
nocturnus, nocturna, nocturnum –
  nocturnal, by night
nōdāre – knot, tie back: nōdat,
  nōdāvit, nōdātus
Nomadēs, Nomadum, m.pl. – the
  Nomads, the Numidians
nōmen, nōminis, n. – name
nōn – not
nōndum – not yet
noster, nostra, nostrum – our
nōtus, nōta, nōtum – known,
  familiar
novāre – make new, renew: novat,
  novāvit, novātus
novus, nova, novum – new
  novissimus, novissima, novissimum
  – last
nox, noctis, f. – night
nūllus, nūlla, nūllum – no, not any
num – *asks a question expecting the
  answer 'no'*
nūmen, nūminis, n. – divine power,
  regard
numquam – never

61

nunc – now
nūsquam – nowhere
nūtrīx, nūtrīcis, f. – nurse
Nymphae, Nymphārum, f.pl. – Nymphs,
demi-goddesses of the wild

O

ō – O!
obitus, obitūs, m. – death, end
oblītus, oblīta, oblītum + Form D
(genitive) – forgetting, heedless of
obmūtēscere – be struck dumb:
obmūtēscit, obmūtuit
obnīxus, obnīxa, obnīxum – struggling,
after a struggle
obortus, oborta, obortum – risen up,
welling up
obscūrus, obscūra, obscūrum –
darkened, dim, pale
Ōceanus, Ōceanī, m. – the Ocean
ōcius – more swiftly
oculus, oculī, m. – eye
ōdisse – hate: ōdit
odium, odiī, n. – hatred
odōrus, odōra, odōrum – keen-scented
ōlim – once
Olympus, Olympī, m. – Mount Olympus
ōmen, ōminis, n. – omen
omnīnō – completely, wholly
omnipotēns – almighty: omnipotentis
omnis, omnis, omne – all, every
operīre – cover: operit, operuit,
opertus
opēs, opum, f.pl. – wealth
optāre – wish, prefer, long for: optat,
optāvit, optātus
optimus, optima, optimum – best,
dear
opus, operis, n. – deed, work
pl. building operations
ōrāre – beg, implore: ōrat, ōrāvit
Orcus, Orcī, m. – Orcus, god of the
Underworld
orgia, orgiōrum, n.pl. – rites
os, ossis, n. – bone
ōs, ōris, n. – mouth, face, expression,
presence, manner

ostentāre – show: ostentat, ostentāvit,
ostentātus
ostrum, ostrī, n. – purple
ōtium, ōtiī, n. – leisure, idleness, time

P

pallēns – pale: pallentis
pallidus, pallida, pallidum – pale
parāre – prepare: parat, parāvit,
parātus
parēns, parentis, m.f. – parent
pārēre + Form C (dative) – obey:
pāret, pāruit
pars, partis, f. – part, side
parvulus, parvula, parvulum – tiny,
dear small
passim – in all directions
pāstor, pāstōris, m. – shepherd
patēns – open: patentis
pater, patris, m. – father
pl. elders, nobles
patera, paterae, f. – bowl
patī – allow: patitur, passus est
patria, patriae, f. – homeland
patrius, patria, patrium – a father's,
ancestral
paucus, pauca, paucum – a few
paulum – a little
pāx, pācis, f. – peace
pectus, pectoris, n. – breast, chest
pecus, pecoris, n. – herd
pecus, pecudis, f. – animal
penātēs, penātium, m.pl. – household
gods, home
pendēre – hang, be suspended: pendet,
pependit
penna, pennae, f. – wing
per + Form B (accusative) – through,
among, by
peragere – finish, complete: peragit,
perēgit, perāctus
peragrāre – roam through: peragrat,
peragrāvit
percutere – strike: percutit, percussit,
percussus
pererrāre – wander over: pererrat,
pererrāvit

perficere – carry through, perform:
perficit, perfēcit, perfectus
perfidus, perfida, perfidum – faithless
Pergama, Pergamōrum, n.pl. – Troy
perīre – die, perish; perit, periit
permittere – allow, hand over, commit:
permittit, permīsit, permissus
pertaedēre + Form D (genitive) – be
weary of: pertaedet, pertaesum est
petere – seek, make for, go for: petit,
petīvit, petītus
pharetra, pharetrae, f. – quiver
Phoebēus, Phoebēa, Phoebēum – of
Apollo, the sun-god
Phoebus, Phoebī, m. – the god Apollo
Phoenissus, Phoenissa, Phoenissum –
Phoenician
Phrygius, Phrygia, Phrygium – Phrygian,
Trojan
piāculum, piāculī, n. – atonement
offering
pictus, picta, pictum – painted
pigēre – regret: piget, piguit
mē piget – I regret, feel sad
pinguis, pinguis, pingue – well-fed,
rich
pius, pia, pium – good, dutiful, holy
placidus, placida, placidum – calm,
peaceful
plaga, plagae, f. – snare
plangor, plangōris, m. – wailing
planta, plantae, f. – sole of foot, foot
plūrimus – see multus
poena, poenae, f. – punishment
Poenī, Poenōrum, m.pl. – the
Carthaginians
polus, polī, m. – axis, sky
pōnere – place, put: pōnit, posuit,
positus
populus, populī, m. – people
porta, portae, f. – gate
portāre – carry: portat, portāvit,
portātus
portus, portūs, m. – harbour
poscere – demand: poscit, poposcit
posse – be able: potest, potuit

post + Form B (accusative) – after
post – afterwards
posterus, postera, posterum – of the
next day
postquam – after
potior, potior, potius – more powerful,
better
praeclārus, praeclāra, praeclārum –
famous
praesentīre – have a presentiment of,
sense: praesentit, praesēnsit,
praesēnsus
praetegere – conceal: praetegit,
praetēxit, praetēxtus
praetendere – hold out, make a
pretence of: praetendit, praetendit,
praetentus
praeterīre – pass, overtake: praeterit,
praeteriit, (praeteritūrus)
precārī – pray: precātur, precātus est
precēs, precum, f.pl. – prayers
premere – press, press down, hide,
cover: premit, pressit, pressus
Priamus, Priamī, m. – Priam,
king of Troy
prīmum – first, for the first time
quam prīmum – as soon as
possible
ut prīmum – as soon as
prīmus, prīma, prīmum – first
prīmī, prīmōrum, m.pl. – nobles,
leaders
prīncipiō – in the beginning, first
prior, prior, prius – former
prius – sooner
prō + Form A (nominative) – in the
name of, by
+ Form E (ablative) – for
prōcēdere – advance: prōcēdit,
prōcessit, (prōcessūrus)
procul – from a distance, in the
distance
profārī – say, speak: profātur,
profātus est
profundus, profunda, profundum
– deep

63

prōgredī – come forward: prōgreditur,
  prōgressus est
prōmerērī – deserve, be deserving:
  prōmerētur, prōmeritus est
prōnuba, prōnubae, f. – bride's
  sponsor
properāre – hurry: properat,
  properāvit
propter + Form B (accusative) –
  because of
prōpugnāculum, prōpugnāculī, n. –
  rampart
Prōserpina, Prōserpinae, f. – Proserpina,
  goddess of death
pudor, pudōris, m. – conscience, sense
  of shame
puer, puerī, m. – boy
pugna, pugnae, f. – fight
pugnāre – fight: pugnat, pugnāvit
pugnus, pugnī, m. – fist
pulcher, pulchra, pulchrum – beautiful
pulverulentus, pulverulenta,
  pulverulentum – dusty
purpureus, purpurea, purpureum –
  purple
Pygmaliōn, Pygmaliōnis, m. –
  Pygmalion, brother of Dido

Q

quaerere – search for, seek: quaerit,
  quaesīvit, quaesītus
quālis, quālis, quāle – just like, like
quam – how, than
  quam prīmum – as soon as possible
quamquam – although
quandō – when, since
quater – four times
-que – and
querēla, querēlae, f. – complaint
querī – complain about: queritur,
  questus est
quī, quae, quod – who, which: cuius
quia – because
quīcumque, quaecumque, quod-
  cumque – whoever, whichever
quid? – why? how?

quiēs, quiētis, f. – rest
quiētus, quiēta, quiētum – calm,
  peaceful
quīn etiam – moreover, worse still
quis, quid – any, anyone, anything:
  cuius
quis, quid? – who, what?: cuius
quisquam, quicquam – anyone,
  anything
quondam – once
quoniam – since
quotiēns – whenever

R

rapere – snatch, hurry: rapit, rapuit,
  raptus
rārus, rāra, rārum – scattered
ratis, ratis, f. – ship
recēdere – pass away: recēdit, recessit
recidīvus, recidīva, recidīvum – restored
recipere – receive, exact: recipit, recēpit,
  receptus
poenās recipere – exact punishment
reclūdere – unsheathe, draw (a sword):
  reclūdit, reclūsit, reclūsus
  reclūsus, reclūsa, reclūsum –
  opened up, open
recursāre – run back, return: recursat,
  recursāvit
redūcere – lead back, rescue: redūcit,
  redūxit, reductus
refellere – argue against: refellit,
  refellit
referre – bear, bring back, recall,
  reply: refert, rettulit, relātus
regere – command, direct: regit,
  rēxit, rēctus
rēgīna, rēgīnae, f. – queen
rēgnātor, rēgnātōris, m. – ruler
rēgnum, rēgnī, n. – kingdom
relinquere – leave: relinquit, relīquit,
  relictus
rēliquiae, rēliquiārum, f.pl. – remains,
  relics
rēmex, rēmigis, m. –rower
rēmus, rēmī, m. – oar

reperīre – find: reperit, repperit,
repertus
repōnere – place carefully: repōnit,
reposuit, repositus
rēs, reī, f. – affair, matter, action
reservāre – save, keep: reservat,
reservāvit, reservātus
resistere – stop, stop short; resistit,
restitit
resolvere – loosen, break: resolvit,
resolvit, resolūtus
resonāre – resound: resonat, resonuit
respicere – consider: respicit, respexit,
respectus
restāre – remain: restat, restitit
rēte, rētis, n. – net
revīsere – return to: revīsit, revīsit,
revīsus
revolvī – roll back: revolvitur, revolūtus
est
rīte – in due fashion
rogus, rogī, m. – funeral pyre
Rōmānus, Rōmāna, Rōmānum –
Roman
rōscidus, rōscida, rōscidum – dewy
ruere – rush, rush out, fall,
be destroyed: ruit, ruit
rumpere – break, break off: rumpit,
rūpit, ruptus
rursus – again

S
sacer, sacra, sacrum – sacred
sacrum, sacrī, n. – sacred emblem,
sacred rite
saepe – often
saevīre – rage: saevit, saeviit
sagitta, sagittae, f. – arrow
saltem – at least
saltus, saltūs, m. – thicket
sanguineus, sanguinea, sanguineum –
bloody, bloodshot
sanguis, sanguinis, m. – blood
sānus, sāna, sānum – healthy, sane
Sāturnius, Sāturniī, m. – descended
from Saturn

saucius, saucia, saucium – wounded,
hurt
saxum, saxī, n. – rock
scēptrum, scēptrī, n. – sceptre
scīlicet – no doubt, I suppose
scopulus, scopulī, m. – rock
sē – himself, herself
sēcum = cum sē
secāre – cut: secat, secuit, sectus
sed – but
sedēre – sit, be settled: sedet, sēdit
sēdēs, sēdis, f. – seat, home
sēdūcere – separate: sēdūcit, sēdūxit,
sēductus
sēgnis, sēgnis, sēgne – sluggish
sēmianimis, sēmianimis, sēmianime –
half-conscious
sēnsus, sēnsūs, m. – feeling
sententia, sententiae, f. – opinion,
plan
sentīre – feel, realise: sentit, sēnsit,
sēnsus
sepulcrum, sepulcrī, n. – tomb, grave
sequī – follow: sequitur, secūtus est
Serestus, Serestī, m. – Serestus, companion of Aeneas
Sergestus, Sergestī, m. – Sergestus,
companion of Aeneas
sermō, sermōnis, m. – speech
servāre – keep: servat, servāvit,
servātus
sēsē = sē
sī – if
sīc – thus
siccāre – dry: siccat, siccāvit, siccātus
Sīdonius, Sīdonia, Sīdonium – from
Sidon
sīdus, sīderis, n. – star, season
signum, signī, n. – sign, signal
silva, silvae, f. – wood
sine + Form E (ablative) – without
sinere – allow: sinit, sīvit, situs
sinus, sinūs, m. – bosom, fold of dress
sistere – place in position, fetch: sistit, stitit
sociāre – join: sociat, sociāvit, sociātus
socius, sociī, m. – companion

sōl, sōlis, m. – sun
sōlārī – console: sōlātur, sōlātus est
sollicitāre – disturb: sollicitat,
    sollicitāvit, sollicitātus
sōlus, sōla, sōlum – alone
solvere – loosen, release: solvit,
    solvit, solūtus
somnus, somnī, m. – sleep
    in somnīs – in a dream
sonāre – make a noise, clash: sonat,
    sonuit
sonipēs, sonipedis, m. – horse, steed
soror, sorōris, f. – sister
sors, sortis, f. – lot, oracle
spargere – scatter, sprinkle, bespatter:
    spargit, sparsit, sparsus
spatiārī – walk solemnly: spatiātur,
    spatiātus est
speciēs, speciēī, f. – outward appearance
specula, speculae, f. – vantage point
spēlunca, spēluncae, f. – cave
spērāre – expect, hope: spērat, spērāvit
spernere – scorn: spernit, sprēvit,
    sprētus
spēs, speī, f. – hope
spīrāre – breathe, live: spīrat, spīrāvit
spīritus, spīritūs, m. – breath, life
sponte – of one's own accord
spūmāns – foaming: spūmantis
stāre – stand: stat, stetit
statuere – build, found: statuit, statuit,
    statūtus
stēllātus, stēllāta, stēllātum – starred,
    studded
stimulāre – spur on: stimulat,
    stimulāvit, stimulātus
stīpāre – crowd round: stīpat, stīpāvit,
    stīpātus
stirps, stirpis, f. – stock, descendants
strāta, strātōrum, n.pl. – coverings,
    couch
strīdere – hiss, sigh: strīdit, strīdit
struere – plan, build: struit, strūxit,
    strūctus
studium, studiī, n. – eagerness
Stygius, Stygia, Stygium – of the
    Underworld

suādēre – persuade, invite: suādet,
    suāsit, (suāsūrus)
sub + Form B (accusative) – under,
    beneath
    + Form E (ablative) – beneath, in
    the depths of
subīre – undertake, support: subit,
    subiit, (subitūrus)
subitus, subita, subitum – sudden
subnectere – fasten: subnectit,
    subnexuit, subnexus
subolēs, subolis, f. – child
succēdere + Form C (dative) – arrive,
    enter: succēdit, successit
succumbere + Form C (dative) – give
    way to: succumbit, succubuit
sūmere – take, adopt: sūmit, sūmpsit,
    sūmptus
summus, summa, summum – highest,
    topmost
super – above, in addition
superī, superōrum, m.pl. – the powers
    above
supplicium, suppliciī, n. – punishment
suprā + Form B (accusative) – above
surgere – rise, grow up: surgit, surrēxit,
    surrēctus
suscipere – undertake, take up, conceive:
    suscipit, suscēpit, susceptus
suspēnsus, suspēnsa, suspēnsum –
    anxious, on edge
suus, sua, suum – his, her, its
Sychaeus, Sychaeī, m. – Sychaeus,
    Dido's first husband
T
tacitus, tacita, tacitum – silent, secret
taeda, taedae, f. – wedding-torch
tālis, tālis, tāle – such
tamen – however
tandem – at length
tangere – touch, reach: tangit, tetigit,
    tāctus
tantum – only
tantus, tanta, tantum – so much, so
    great
tēctum, tēctī, n. – roof, shelter, house
tegere – cover: tegit, texit, tēctus

tēla, tēlae, f. – thread
tellūs, tellūris, f. – earth
tēlum, tēlī, n. – weapon, spear
tempora, temporum, n.pl. – brow
temptāre – try: temptat, temptāvit,
    temptātus
tempus, temporis, n. – time
tenēre – hold, restrain: tenet, tenuit,
    tentus
tenuis, tenuis, tenue – thin, fine
ter – three times
terere – rub, waste (time): terit, trīvit,
    trītus
terminus, terminī, m. – boundary
    stone, limit
terra, terrae, f. – earth, land, country,
    the world
terrēre – frighten: terret, terruit,
    territus
testārī – swear by: testātur, testātus est
tetigit – see tangere
Teucrī, Teucrōrum, m.pl. – the Trojans
thalamus, thalamī, m. – room, bridal
    chamber
Thȳias, Thȳiadis, f. – a Maenad, a
    follower of Bacchus
tigris, tigris, m.f. – tiger
timēre – fear: timet, timuit
timor, timōris, m. – fear
Tīthōnus, Tīthōnī, m. – Tithonus,
    Aurora's husband
torquēre – twist: torquet, torsit, tortus
torus, torī, m. – couch
tōtus, tōta, tōtum – whole
trādere – surrender: trādit, trādidit,
    trāditus
trahere – drag, draw after: trahit,
    trāxit, tractus
trānsmittere – cross: trānsmittit,
    trānsmīsit, trānsmissus
tremēns – trembling, quivering:
    trementis
trepidus, trepida, trepidum – agitated,
    trembling
trietēricus, trietērica, trietēricum –
    held in alternate years
trivium, triviī, n. – crossroads

Troiānus, Troiāna, Troiānum – Trojan
tū, tuī – you
tuērī – watch: tuētur
tulit – see ferre
tum – then
turbidus, turbida, turbidum – disturbed,
    unquiet
turris, turris, f. – tower
tūtus, tūta, tūtum – safe, secure
tuus, tua, tuum – your
tyrannus, tyrannī, m. – ruler
Tyriī, Tyriōrum, m.pl. – the Tyrians
Tyrius, Tyria, Tyrium – from Tyre,
    Phoenician
Tyros, Tyrī, f. – Tyre

U

ūber, ūberis, n. – udder
ubi – where, when
ultor, ultōris, m. – avenger
ultrīx – avenging: ultrīcis
ultrō – of one's own accord
ultus, ulta, ultum – having avenged
ululāre – howl (for), cry out: ululat,
    ululāvit, ululātus
ululātus, ululātūs, m. – crying
umbra, umbrae, f. – shadow, darkness,
    ghost, shade
ūmēns – dank: ūmentis
umerus, umerī, m. – shoulder
umquam – ever
ūnā – at the same time
ūnanimus, ūnanima, ūnanimum – of
    one mind, dearly loved
unda, undae, f. – wave
undōsus, undōsa, undōsum – full of
    waves, surging
unguis, unguis, m. – finger-nail
ūnus, ūna, ūnum – one: ūnius
urbs, urbis, f. – city
ūrere – burn: ūrit, ussit, ustus
ūsus, ūsūs, m. – use, purpose
ut + indicative – as, when
ut + subjunctive – that, so that
uterque, utraque, utrumque – each
    (of two)
uxōrius – under a wife's sway

67

V

vacca, vaccae, f. – cow

vacuus, vacua, vacuum – empty

vagārī – wander: vagātur, vagātus est

valēre – be well, be able: valet, valuit

vallis, vallis, f. – valley

vānus, vāna, vānum – groundless, without reason

varius, varia, varium – varied, different

vātēs, vātis, m.f. – soothsayer, priest

–ve – or

vel – or

   vel...vel – either...or

velle – wish, want, be willing: vult, voluit

vēlum, vēlī, n. – sail

vēna, vēnae, f. – vein

vēnābulum, vēnābulī, n. – hunting-spear

venīre – come: venit, vēnit, (ventūrus)

ventus, ventī, m. – wind

Venus, Veneris, f. – the goddess Venus

verbum, verbī, n. – word

vērō – indeed

versāre – turn about: versat, versāvit, versātus

vertex, verticis, m. – summit, top of the head

vērum – but

vestīgium, vestīgiī, n. – trace

vestis, vestis, f. – garment, dress

vetus – old: veteris

vexāre – trouble: vexat, vexāvit, vexātus

vicissim – in turn

victus, victa, victum – conquered, overcome

vidēre – see: videt, vīdit, vīsus

vidērī – seem: vidētur, vīsus est

vinclum = vinculum

vinculum, vinculī, n. – bond

violāre – violate, dishonour: violat, violāvit, violātus

vir, virī, m. – man, husband

virtūs, virtūtis, f. – courage

vīs, f. – strength

   pl. vīrēs – power

vīsus, vīsūs, m. – sight

vīta, vītae, f. – life

vitta, vittae, f. – garland

vīvere – live: vīvit, vīxit, (vīctūrus)

vocāre – call, summon: vocat, vocāvit, vocātus

volātilis, volātilis, volātile – winged

volvere – roll, dart: volvit, volvit, volūtus

vōs – you

vōtum, vōtī, n. – prayer, offering

vōx, vōcis, f. – voice

vulnus, vulneris, n. – wound

vultus, vultūs, m. – face, expression

X

Xanthus, Xanthī, m. – the river Xanthus in Lycia